UnHoly Communion

EXPANDED EDITION

LESSONS LEARNED FROM LIFE AMONG PEDOPHILES, PREDATORS, AND PRIESTS

HANK ESTRADA

Red Rabbit Press LLC

New Mexico

2nd edition—2021

1st edition—2011

ISBN 10: 0-9740988-5-2

ISBN 13: 978-0-974098852

New Mexico, USA

PRAISES FOR UnHoly Communion

"An important contribution to the field and will be an example of one more male survivor who is powerful and demonstrates that recovery is absolutely possible and achievable!"

—Howard Fradkin, Ph.D., Psychologist

"This is an important story! A great deal to say that can be of great help to victims and for the betterment of the church and society."

—Richard Sipe, Author, Sex, Priests, and Secret Codes

"An emotionally charged journey. The juxtaposition of religious chaos is compelling. Powerful in its genuine open and powerful truthfulness."

—Christian Crawford, Author, Mommie Dearest

"Very compelling, very disturbing, very well done!"

—David Clohessy, Former Co-Founder & National Director, SNAP (Survivors Network of those Abused by Priests)

DEDICATION

To all those individuals in relationships with an adult survivor of childhood abuse. Thank you for your patience and understanding when our survivor issues become THE issue. When our unexpressed emotional pain unintentionally hurts you, and when our lack of intimacy makes you feel lonely. We are grateful for your tolerance, patience, and loving support. And finally, to my life partner Antonio, whose unconditional love for me since September 11, 1983, is my most cherished and sacred blessing in this life.

ACKNOWLEDGMENTS

I wish to thank the following individuals, especially

for their support and assistance:

Richard Sipe

David Clohessy

Christina Crawford

CONTENTS

PREFACE

In 1985 I reluctantly and publicly "came out" on a local morning television talk show as one of the first adult male survivors of incest. That same year, while living in Los Angeles, California, I found myself forming a nonprofit organization for non-offending adult male survivors of child sexual abuse, another first. Then I self-published Recovery for Male Victims of Child Sexual Abuse, a book about my recovery journey. Following subsequent years of intense public advocacy work, I eventually realized and accepted the purpose for my humiliating molestation disclosure with tremendous gratitude. I was finally able to confidently enjoy the emotional peace of not having to talk about being a survivor of incest and child abuse or about my personal "healing" journey.

Approximately nineteen years later, in the spring of 2004, while I was living contently in northern New Mexico; I felt my sense of personal security suddenly challenged by yet another sexual assault, a psychological trauma I thought I had conquered and buried long ago. I learned of a Southern California man who alleged that a Catholic priest whom he sought out for spiritual direction had seduced him.

I discovered that the priest he identified as his perpetrator was the the same priest who, in the late 1970s, had sexually assaulted me while I was in college and a Catholic seminarian under his supervision. Admittedly I was shocked, angered, and upset to hear a complete stranger tell me, in very familiar detail, how Father John Raab, C.M.F., a Roman Catholic priest, had seduced him with friendship, trust, and intimate gestures of affection. I had never spoken publicly about this experience to anyone; but now I realize I simply have no other choices but to do so.

As of this printing, Father John Raab, C.M.F., remains an ordained priest with the Claretian Missionary Order in Los Angeles, where we first met. What follows here is painfully honest and intimate story of this survivor's lifelong battle against pedophiles, a sexual predator priest, and those who protect them.

Approximately two weeks before the release of UnHoly Communion, I received a phone call from someone identifying himself as an attorney representing the Claretian Missionary Order and stated that he wanted to discuss a settlement offer. I don't know how the Claretian Order knew that UnHoly Communion was about to be release, especially since I did not have any verbal or written contact with any of them.

After reporting Fr. Raab to his superiors, the thought of filing or pursuing legal actions against Fr. Rabb or the Claretian Order was never a consideration. So, to suddenly receive this mysterious settlement proposal phone call was shocking, to say the least. I immediately felt that I was being bribed into stopping the release of UnHoly Communion. I rejected the proposal and terminated the call. To this day, I have no idea how they even knew about my book or that it was about to be released.

INTRODUCTION

I was 23 years old in 1979 when Father John Raab sexually assaulted me. I was assigned to Saint Anne's Parish in Fort Worth, Texas as a seminarian and placed under his leadership and spiritual supervision. During that time, Father John (as I called him) skillfully and knowingly proceeded to psychologically groom me for weeks leading up to an actual physical seduction, followed by repeated sexual assaults thereafter.

Not long after the sexual contact had ended between Father John and me, I confronted him and suggested he get psychological counseling. I also reported him to several of his Claretian superiors, who assured me that my concerns would be addressed immediately. I was also informed by the Provincial, an ordained priest elected as superior of the Religious Order, that Father John would never again be assigned to supervise or work directly with students or seminarians on any level. I felt relieved and comforted that I had identified Father John as someone to be watched. I also believed these religious superiors when they assured me he would get the appropriate psychological counseling necessary to stop any further inappropriate physical behavior or sexual assaults.

The painful truth is that I eventually discovered that Father John's superiors simply reassigned him to yet another position, this time, overseas to a Claretian mission in Africa where he was once again given a supervisory position over new young seminarians. Apparently, they just moved him from one assignment to another without ever directly addressing his compulsive sexual behavior issues or getting him appropriate psychological counseling.

After having alerted several other Claretian Missionary priests, including the Religious Orders Provincial, I learned that little had been done over the years to protect others from Father John's inappropriate physical behavior and sexual advances. I have had to face the fact that information regarding Father John's predatory behavior has continued to resurface throughout various periods of my adult life. I've now recommitted myself to undertake the challenges of confronting sexual predator clergy and those who protect them. In my opinion, the fact that sexual predator priests remain active ministers, somewhere in the world is a more seriously disturbing threat today then my own childhood perpetrator ever was.

As you will read, I, too, am not without fault, weaknesses, or compulsions. Unfortunately, like most survivors of sexual assaults and abuse, I am my own harshest critic when it comes to personal indiscretions and compulsions. I remain capable of occasionally making poor choices regarding personal associations, relationships, and intimacy. I have accepted the fact that much of the significant early childhood influences in my life have revolved around unhealthy addictive behaviors, i.e., chemical dependency and sexual compulsiveness.

Despite everything I've experienced in my life thus far, I am resolved to do the best I can with whatever tempting or threatening circumstances I face. More importantly, when I fail in my struggles to overcome risky compulsive behavior, I can now recall just what type of situations trigger unhealthy responses, evaluate which specific factors influence my decisions and focus on identifying positive alternatives. When similar urges resurface, and they always do, I take what I've learned from each past decision, no matter how painful or uncomfortable, to avoid repeating those with the most humiliating and unhealthy consequences.

I do not, by any means, hold "the key" to complete healing and recovery, but I know from experience what helps me and what does not. It's my desire to share with you the reoccurring subconscious triggers and behavioral responses that I, as a sexual abuse survivor, have faced since my experiences first began as a five-year-old boy. I also never assume that my experiences are unique or isolated. Many adult survivors struggle daily with similar circumstances and issues. I'm but one of many who have survived traumatic sexual abuse experiences, most as children and now as an adult survivor at the hands of a sexual predator priest.

After my first book, Recovery for Male Victims of Child Sexual Abuse, I never imagined I'd be writing a second book all these years later, this time as an adult survivor of clergy sexual abuse. I'm thankfully aware that I cannot and will not keep silent about these equally horrendous sexual predator crimes by religious clergy committed against innocent people of faith. I pledge here, once again, to diligently use my single voice to publicly seek justice for today's still invisible and silent survivors of abuse by sexual predators.

CHAPTER 1

"GO TO HELL"

"Go to hell" is a reference to my many years of Catholic religious education, Sunday sermons, and moral indoctrination regarding "good" and "evil" behavior. We were then and still, in some communities, taught that "evil" behavior assures individual souls will go to "hell." When "they" (church authorities and clergy) spoke of damnation and "hell," we lay people listened and allowed fear to rule our personal decisions and conduct. The ultimate fear for the faithful would be existence in hell for all eternity. It's clear that the religious faithful still lives their lives attempting to avoid the damnation of disobedience as prescribed by religious authority.

In January 2002, the Boston Globe published an article that broke the Catholic Church's shameful secret of actively protecting known pedophile clergy from unsuspecting parishioners. The article clearly demonstrated that the church authorities had decided, long ago, to simply relocate a priest from his parish whenever an accusation of molestation was brought against him. The new parish and its parishioners were never warned about the newly assigned priest's predatory history and fell victim to his physical, emotional, and sexual assaults time and time again. When this devastating clergy sex abuse scandal broke, many survivors felt that the clergy perpetrators were surely going to go to "hell." Of course, Catholic Church officials were quick to defend themselves by angrily confronting victims who bravely came forward to speak out. Many of these church officials were even quicker to hire top-dollar attorneys to discredit and morally destroy former victimized parishioners who sought church protection and support. The horrendous confrontations between victims and church officials and their attorneys continue today without much media attention in communities across the country. It remains my opinion that every person, religious or otherwise, who knew of or participated in sexual molestations, deserves to go to the "hell" we were constantly threatened with.

When I was a young Catholic seminarian, the fear of "hell" took on a more academic and philosophic understanding. For me, "hell" was no longer fire and brimstone but an eternal existence of suffering and inescapable misery. Still, I recall hearing from several religious superiors that "hell" was a viable consequence for "evil" behavior, most notable expressions of physical love between adults of the same sex and divorced couples who remarry.

All the while, Catholic bishops, cardinals, and the Pope contributed to the sexual corruption and victimization of thousands of spiritually faithful parishioners. They secretly continued to transfer pedophile priests from one parish to another without warning the new community. Sometimes the sexual predator priest was assigned to a temporary secret psychological treatment center for offenders, often without measurably rehabilitative results before being reassigned. This unforgivable practice comes as no surprise in light of the fact that every Catholic cardinal takes an oath never divulge anything confided to him that "might bring harm or dishonor to Holy Mother Church."

Still today, many organized religions use the prospect of "hell" to sway and manipulate their congregations. Ultimately, it is not up to any one faith, clergyperson, or spiritual leader to say who will or will not go to "hell." For those religious zealots and hypocrites who insist on relying on verbal assaults, protest demonstrations, bible verse quoting, and physical violence, I'm comforted in my belief that these individuals will be first among those who indeed should "Go to Hell"

I believe that only the God one believes in can decide what happens to us after we die. It is also my opinion that every organized religion is susceptible to having morally corrupt hypocrites among faithful followers, even more so among those in positions of power. What those who call themselves spiritual leaders have failed to learn time and time again is to first give up their own secrets and sin-filled lives before preaching "hell" to the rest of us.

Adults Seduced by Clergy

Much about clergy sexual abuse reported in recent years involve priests who molested young children. However, clergy abuse doesn't just happen to children. Abuse can also be inflicted upon adults: adult survivors of child sexual abuse coerced into multiple sexual encounters by predator clergy who claim temporal or spiritual power over them, exactly what took place between Father John Rabb and me. It is my hope that sharing this experience will help adult survivors who were sexually assaulted as adults by sexual predator clergy to find courage, hope, and the inspiration to speak out. These predators have to be confronted and stopped at every opportunity, particularly by survivors like us.

Unfortunately, many remain silent because they have witnessed the overwhelming emotional battles between victims/survivors of clergy abuse and large organized religious institutions like the Catholic Church. I understand that not every victim/survivor of sexual abuse, regardless of who the perpetrator was, is capable of openly and publicly standing up to tell their story.

Not every survivor thinks equally regarding confronting their perpetrator, publicly speaking out, seeking justice, or in some matters, receiving compensation from their perpetrators. Each of us has to find that particular place of personal justice and peace with regards to healing and recovery.

For those who simply cannot come forward for whatever reason, I understand their fears and apprehensions and hope this book moves them to advocate beyond themselves for the sake of others. You have to know and understand that you are not your perpetrator's one and only victim. The fact of the matter is, sexual predators and pedophiles have sexually assaulted others before you and, most likely, have moved on to molest others after you.

CHAPTER 2

RELIGIOUS VOCATION

In 1972, at the age of 16, I had reached a point in my young life of absolute hopelessness and overwhelming feelings of emptiness and saw no escape from the psychological terror of living with the violent outburst of an alcoholic father and the manipulative seductions of his sexually abusive brother, Uncle Oscar. I had no one to talk to, no one to rescue me; suicide seemed my only way out. I hated myself and the abusive home in which I lived. I was sickened, confused, and disturbed by two issues: that my uncle Oscar was mentally coercing me to have frequent sex with him in my house and that my body responded with pleasure to his physical stimulation. I existed in a state of self-conscious distress and mental confusion.

One day in 1974, during my senior year of high school, in a moment of desperation, I locked myself in the bathroom with a razor blade in one hand, standing before the vanity, ready to slice my wrists. Tears ran down my cheeks. Excruciating hours of depression and sadness had led to this moment, and I could not think of one person, important enough in my life to want to live for or who loved me unconditionally and without impossible expectations. In a split second, before slicing my vein, I froze.

Somehow I experienced an unexpected moment of insight and hope. My thoughts had turned to the comfort that spiritual focus brings, and I was unable to follow through with the horrible task of killing myself. As a practicing Catholic, I thought that it must have been God who prevented me from actually taking my life that day. And that God must have some reason, some purpose for keeping me

9

alive. It was this thought that led me to believe I might have a special calling to do something important, something I couldn't understand right then.

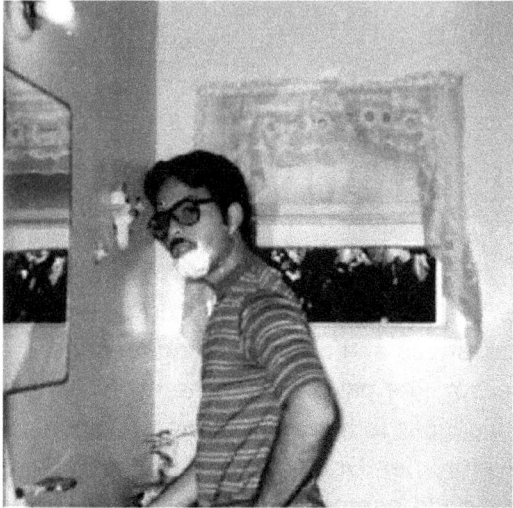

At 16, suicide was attempted at this very spot.

In my mind, as I stood in the bathroom, it struck me that the most honorable way for a Catholic to give his life over to completely God was to become a priest, and so I began making inquiries. I spoke with my local priest, who advised that, in addition to seeking therapy, I start to read scripture, attend bible study classes and spiritual retreats, and speak with various clergy. Following his advice, I threw myself into my religious studies and prayed frequently, all the while feeling more and more hopeful and confident in this new direction for my life. I felt further drawn into the religious life after attending several seminary vocation exploration retreats.

In the fall of 1974, I entered the Catholic religious order of the Claretian Missionary Priests and Brothers and began seminary training to become a priest. I was 18 years old. My family and friends were completely surprised at my decision to pursue the religious life of a priest but supported me as best they knew how. I was finally out of a truly terrifying, turbulent, and abusive childhood home life, safely on my own now and out of harm's way, or so I thought.

10

I joined the Western Province of the Claretian Missionaries order in Los Angeles, California. I was particularly attracted to this order because the Claretians are devoted to social concerns and issues of justice and peace in parishes and foreign missions, magazine publishing, and serving more than sixty countries on five continents. I had researched and interviewed several religious communities, as well as the Los Angeles Diocesan seminary, but was drawn to this particular community by the actual priests and brothers I had met and conversed with me.

The order's founder, Saint Anthony Mary Claret, encouraged his Missionaries to "use all possible means for the salvation of souls" and this is what I saw the Claretians creatively doing. They were smart, witty, committed ordinary men taking on extraordinary causes, such as supporting Cesar Chavez and the United Farm Workers boycotts, helping establish social justice programs and staffing many foreign missions. Working predominately in Latino and African American communities, the Claretians seemed to be involved with neighborhoods that needed the most work, both spiritually and economically.

I was excited about my decision to join this community of priests and brothers because I now felt that I could embrace a new life of prayer, service, and inner peace. I had renewed enthusiasm for my life as a servant of God in the Catholic Church. Having spent much of my childhood living in dread and fear, I felt all that seemingly disappear with each new Claretian Priest or Brother I was introduced to.

An important part of the Claretian seminarian training was for new seminarians to attend public school institutions, gaining education , and performing volunteer work at local parishes. We gathered around 5 p.m. for daily Mass, followed by a communal dinner and great discussions and debates on any number of topics. I enjoyed these interactions and cherished those moments of mental expression and exchange. Evenings were usually spent studying, and at 9 p.m. we would gather once again for evening prayers before retiring for bed. The schedule would repeat itself throughout the academic school year. Every summer, after the semester ended, each seminarian was assigned a summer post for further hands-on ministry training and placed under the supervision and spiritual direction of a senior priest.

I gained tremendous personal support from my superiors and spiritual directors during these assignment periods.

For the first time in my 18 years of life, I was able to talk openly with my religious superiors about being sexually abused as a child and was encouraged to describe some of the violent, traumatic episodes I had experienced but held as a tightly guarded, personal secret. I felt relieved of the burden and free to express my most intimate fears, thoughts, and feelings. I was never chastised for expressing my anger or silenced in shame. The seminary was a wonderfully caring and supportive learning environment for me. I found my inner voice and gradually learned to express myself more clearly. I was encouraged to speak out bravely and found unlimited acceptance and support. I learned to be confident with public speaking. It was at this time that I realized I could never again remain silent about my childhood sexual abuse experiences, and I began to openly assert, from that time forward and with confidence, that I was an incest survivor.

I was happy to be practicing chastity during seminary training because I had carried so much emotional baggage regarding sex from my childhood. During my childhood, there were many confusing contradictions regarding love, sex, and relationships that were still unresolved within me as a young man. Sex was a confusing element for me, and I was glad not to have to deal with it, to confront it at all. That's what I thought.

Throughout seminary life, I, like most male seminarians, engaged in private moments of masturbation, both as an ongoing temptation but more often as a welcome releasing of stress. Seminarians were encouraged not to masturbate but instead to strive for complete celibacy.However, in reality, there was so much unspoken sexual tension, I personally had to masturbate several times a week just to mentally end my overwhelming preoccupation with it.

There were many times in the seminary—or house of studies as we referred to it — when various sexual topics and conversations would present themselves among us. At times these topics would revolve around romantic relationships, sexual behavior, morality, celibacy, and the like, arising from the social encounters we individually experienced on campus, and some were questions sparked from our spiritual studies. The seminary house had an average of six to nine seminarians, each man sharing a room with one other seminarian.

There was always one Prefect, a priest who served as the house leader. This priest lived in his own room within the house. The Prefect was always available to talk to, and he supervised most of the study activities and our community ministry assignments.

In addition to straight seminarians, several in our house were gay, some bisexual, but all of them closeted. There was comfortableness among us seminarians. We felt free to talk about everything, to bring honesty to our discussions. This was especially true when we were in formal, supervised training sessions. After months of sharing our most intimate thoughts and fears with each other, the majority of us felt safe to continue the personal verbal sharing with one another in private. As might be imagined, on occasion, these discussion topics would turn sexual, and then an awkward nervousness would surface between the two seminarians that could potentially complicate one's practice of celibacy.

Personally, at times I would feel physically aroused by certain forms of playful physical contact and sexual talk with other seminarians, and I was aware that, for the most part, this form of release could only go so far without becoming a problem. The sexual tension definitely existed in the seminary for both straight and gay seminarians, as well as with some senior spiritual advisors, as one would expect in an all-male environment and household.

After my first year in seminary, I understood and accepted that I was born a sexual feeling human being and would forever have to find healthy, appropriate outlets in order to maintain my religious vow of celibacy.

Claretian Seminarians, Los Angeles, CA, 1977. I am seated front row, second from left.

Overall, my seminary studies and experiences were extremely positive, and I worked very hard to follow the vows of poverty, chastity, and obedience. I found seminary life to be a supportive, loving environment and spent hour upon hour in open discussions about myself, my feelings, and my desire to one day become a Catholic priest within the Claretian Missionary Order.Again, having left my violent, abusive childhood home for the safety of the seminary was a welcome relief for me and proved to be life-changing.

Periodically, during the six years, I spent studying for the Catholic priesthood, I was informed of dysfunctional family problems that would surface back home. Because of my new perspective and living situation, I was mentally able to remove myself from any emotional family attachments, in particular from my violent, alcoholic father and his sexually abusive brother. I chose to communicate with my family only within those "manageable" peaceful and calm periods when phone calls and visits were comfortable. Never before had I felt in such control of my life.

Not surprisingly, I kept my distance from most family gatherings during my years of seminary. Conversely, I found constant and steady support from fellow seminarians and spiritual advisors and felt

14

fortunate to have their ongoing acceptance and encouragement. The following letter to my family, which I wrote during my first year, clearly demonstrates the dramatic impact seminary living had on my thinking process:

Dear Mom, Dad, brothers, and sisters, There are many times when, like right now at this retreat, I am left alone to think, to pray, and to just "be." I have had a lot of silent time to reflect. I think and pray a lot about us, on life and everything that is life. I think on how much I've taken things for granted, on how much I didn't understand, sometimes still don't. I think about how we spend our lives, how we treat people as if they're going to be here tomorrow or as if nothing could take them away from us, then I see how wrong an assumption this is. I think of how many times I've wanted to say to you, "I love you," but could only feel it and not say it. I want to tell you now that I truly love you; I always have and always will. I will love you no matter where I am, how far go or in whatever I do—

"I love you, and I need you." I realize this may seem strange for me to write and say, but I say it because I see others who have waited too long to express this and lost the opportunity forever. I don't want to feel sorry for something I never said as I love you but always wanted to. We are growing older, and each one of us will choose his or her own way of living our dreams. I always pray for all of you that we may each come to know what our purpose in this life is and how we can better support and love each other. Always know that it's family and our love that matters, that's all! More important is that God gave us each other to love, if even for a short time. I pray for each of us to be patient, happy, and to feel the experience of true unconditional love. Remember, no matter what may happen, I love you very much. Know that I am happy and feel I belong. I am learning to love more and show love, and I am able to give more of myself out of love. I just needed to let you know that wherever I go. I believe you are there too. With love and prayers for God to bless you, your son and brother, Hank

During my studies as a seminarian when I began to feel more Comfortable with expressing myself, it became clearer to me to accept what I had known in my heart since childhood—that I was gay.

Given this, I now needed to face a new and ever-growing challenge of controlling my attraction to certain individuals who had shown sympathy and understanding towards me, those with whom I had become emotionally intimate. The feeling of acceptance was completely new to me because, before joining the seminary, I had never felt supported or cared for. I instinctively wanted to respond, to act in the only way I had been misguidedly taught to do so as a child by my uncle: through physical intimacy and sex. Not the most appropriate form of expression in an all-male seminary, but up until that time, the only consistent form of intimate sharing I knew.

I struggled, oh how I struggled, to realize that I didn't need to "perform sexually" upon those who praised me or sought my companionship. I had to relearn new and more appropriate manners of responding to genuine affection, friendship, and nonsexual physical touch.

I frequently spoke with spiritual directors and prayed a lot about the confusing struggle taking place within me. I was grateful for my daily successes in maintaining celibacy and was hopeful in controlling future urges. Most of the time, I found that talking openly and frankly about my sexual tension issues helped eliminate much of the seemingly overwhelming temptations I battled with; but naturally, sometimes it didn't.

Despite my understanding, this confused, sexualized way of thinkingremained within me as a major challenge I've continued fighting against unhealthy compulsive behaviors and, eventually, sexual addiction. These two difficulties had yet to fully surface during my early years of seminary training, but indeed they would.

Catholic Priesthood

While living in a religious community of Catholic priests and brothers, I quickly learned about the many personal benefits a religious clergyman receives throughout his priesthood, among them prestige, privilege, protection, and often unchallenged influential power over parishioners. Could these questionable benefits lead to arrogance, self-righteousness, and a false sense of invincibility on the part of the priest? What about a sense of accountability, respect, adherence to morality, protection of the innocent, and being true examples of Christ's presence in the world?

I witnessed as these men who wore a traditional black suit with white "Roman" collar, undeniably the most recognizable symbol of the Catholic priesthood was frequently sought out, pampered, given unlimited trust and attention, and had people constantly offering to do things for them.

Internally, I questioned some priests I saw that took the spiritual "gift" of priesthood and turn it into something they bartered with, a way to control parishioners, as though saying, "If you treat me special, I will pray and give you blessings from our Lord."

"I designed this logo in 1976, and it is still in use today."

Whenever a "Father" offered, well-meaning parents would allow their young sons to sleep over at the rectory or go on overnight outings with priests. Parents would show visible pride knowing their boy was selected from all others and would boast to fellow family and friends about the special attention "Father" bestowed on their sons, not realizing the horrific sexual assaults many would endure. Fortunately, in the United States, families have now learned not to simply hand over their child to clergy members who express a special interest in their child. Unfortunately, however, in numerous foreign countries still today, predator priests and clergy have unlimited access to numerous trusting parents.

Nearly every material need was provided for every priest and seminarian: meals, gas, insurance, medical care, cars, travel expenses, even housing. Priests and religious clergy are the objects of unending attention and attraction by the faithful—and they know it. Even as a seminarian, when I dressed in full black priestly garb with white collar, I noticed and experienced parishioners vying for the opportunity to get physically close to me with ostentatious hugs, overly friendly innuendos, and by initiating private and exclusive one-on-one conversations. There was no way to ignore this typical reaction from people each time they saw me wearing the traditional Roman collar. It remains a tempting fact for all religious persons who wear distinctive clergy-affiliated garb. No doubt, many parishioners still react this way when a priest enters a room wearing his collar.

I vividly remember being taught as a child to look up to the local priest and sternly urged to offer him complete respect and reverence whenever our paths crossed. Never in my entire young life was there any discussion about being careful or cautious around a priest. A priest could do no wrong. I was proud, knowing I was on my own personal journey to becoming an honorable priest. I truly felt without regrets that I was now called to a religious vocation and fortunate enough to be among this friendly community of ordained priests and religious brothers.

As seminarians, we were expected to attend public colleges and select training programs that most interested us academically and socially. The wearing of the Roman collar was permitted only in times when ministry service was being performed around the parish and in hospitals and jail settings. We taught religious education classes, studied liturgy and homily sermon preparation, visited the sick and elderly, and led rosary recitals during wakes and funeral prayer services. Some of us also sang in choirs, and those with musical talents performed with local parish music groups.

Collar pic

The most rewarding choice I made for my ministerial training was to work among persons who were deaf and hearing impaired. I was fortunate enough to be involved with one of the largest Catholic hearing-impaired communities in the Los Angeles Archdiocese and apprenticed under a remarkable hard of hearing priest, Father Brian Doran. With Father Doran's guidance and leadership, I became a sign language interpreter and eventually learned to translate the entire liturgy from Spanish and English into American Sign Language and vice versa, something few interpreters were able to do at the time.

Father Doran remains one of the most dedicated, beloved, and revered priests, for his years of service and personal sacrifice, not only to Catholics with hearing impairments in Southern California, but also among persons with other disabilities in communities across the country.

In 1979 I graduated with a BA from Loyola Marymount University in Los Angeles and was to begin my Masters of Theology training in Berkeley, California, the following September. Shortly after college graduation, I was assigned to spend the summer working at Saint Anne's, a Claretian parish in Fort Worth, Texas.

I was to assist the pastor and his associates with whatever they chose for me to do as part of my seminary pastoral training. There I was introduced to Father John Rabb. He was about ten years older

19

and had been asked to supervise me in various church ministries. He was familiar to me from occasional social encounters at our annual community retreats provided for all priests, brothers, and seminarians within the Claretian Order and at various ceremonial religious events. My first impression of Father John was that he was a quiet, prayerful, and a spiritually sensitive young priest.

Chapter 3

Meeting Father John

Father John Raab quickly took me under his authority and introduced me to everyone in the parish. He often complimented me on my appearance and my "very friendly" smile. I definitely enjoyed the unexpected attention and initially appreciated the compliments. Being alone in a new place or among strangers was slightly uncomfortable, but Father John helped me feel welcomed and appreciated. I began looking forward to receiving Father John's undivided attention and the personal praises he lavished upon me, which continued throughout the summer. Father John struck me as a very gentle, spiritually prayerful, and intelligent man, and I admired his overall sense of serenity and soft tone voice.

One hot summer afternoon after working all weekend with Father John, I was invited to join our parish household for an outing to a nearby lake. All the Claretian priests and brothers from Saint Anne's parish went, including Father John. About four or five of us got into a car and traveled up to Lake San Marcos. Until this outing, I hadn't shared much personal information with Father John or he with me. The majority of our communications had revolved around various ministry activities and parish religious life.

This outing, I thought, would offer me a chance to get to know a little more about Father John—the man, instead of just knowing him as a priest and spiritual mentor. I innocently thought that perhaps I would learn about his personal interests, family life, hobbies, et cetera.

After we had arrived at the lake and were enjoying ourselves in the water, swimming and horsing around, Father John suddenly swam over to me and began splashing me in a frolicking manner. At one point, he playfully grabbed hold of my arm, reached down to seize and tickle my foot, and then pushed my head under the water. When I resurfaced, he tickled me again by placing both his hands around my waist; then he moved his arms up and around my chest and stomach, holding me tightly against his body for a few seconds. A sudden feeling of discomfort surged through my body. I was surprised because I didn't know Father John could be so playful, and yet here he was, touching and grabbing me aggressively. Old, confused feelings of excitement, fear, and pleasure that were familiar from my past once again surface within me. I was torn between feeling excited that Father John was comfortable enough to display his attention on me and ashamed that I was getting physically aroused as well.

I pushed him away and off of me; but instead of taking this as an assertive clue, he came up from behind me and once more pulled me against his body, only this time I could feel his erect penis pressing up against my back. He wore a small bikini, and if he had been standing above water, his penis would have stuck out above the waistband.

I instinctively pushed him away and was shocked that he made no attempt to excuse himself or apologize. I realized then that he was testing to see just how far he could take this sexual escapade. His only reaction was to smile and stare at me as I swam away and got out of the water. I avoided Father John for the rest of the day until we were seated alone together in the back seat of the car for the long drive home to the parish.

We had a five or six-hour drive that late afternoon, and each of us took a turn driving. Those who sat in the rear seat took turns trying to sleep; one would lie down while the other sat up. Towards the last three hours of our trip, the late afternoon turned to dusk, and as it turned out, Father John and I found ourselves in the back seat— alone. I was lying down with my head rested on a sleeping bag near Father John's lap, and at one point, he lifted the sleeping bag away and gently placed my head on his lap.

At first, he did nothing but sit there; then, he began to stroke my hair, very gently and tenderly. It felt unusually comfortable and relaxing. He then placed his hand on my chest, and occasionally he would gently slide it over my chest. I could feel his eyes just studying me as he continued to rub his hand over my arms and chest softly. I remember feeling really safe and cared for, unlike anything I had experienced in childhood.

A few times, I sensed his whole body tense up from wanting to reach down from my stomach to touch my crotch. He would lift his hand from resting on my belly and then gently drop it back down as though he were fighting temptation. I also saw him studying the other two members seated up front, making sure they weren't observing his movements. I felt uneasy, anxious, and once more very confused. I was unsure of many things, which included my religious vocation, self-worth, the magnitude that negative choices and consequences could have for the religious life I was preparing for. I was in a state of distress and quickly sat up, acting as though I had just awakened from sleep, although in reality, I had been totally awake.

Because I knew nothing about Father John's personal history, in my limited way, I was attempting to sort out my own perceptions about him. However, this did no good, and instead, I became more confused than ever. Was he just an extremely "touchy-feely" type of guy, sincere in his affection, or was he really physically and sexually attracted to men—to me? I felt bad as if I had been letting my own sexual abuse history taint this seemingly gentle priest's friendly expressions of physical affection. I was completely at a loss.

Later that same night, when I was getting ready for bed, Father John called me over to his room. I put on my walking shorts and walked to his room, which was located directly across from mine. I found him standing, facing me, wearing only his walking shorts and no shirt, and holding in his hand a tube of sunburn lotion. He asked if I would rub some lotion on his sunburnt back and shoulders. Before I could answer; he quickly stripped off his shorts and fell face down on his bed, wearing only his boxers. I thought it strange that he would remove his pants when all he had asked me to do was rub cream on his shoulders and back, but I, as a young child, always taught or rather programmed to obey authority.

Wanting to get this quickly over with, I spread the lotion over his obviously sunburnt back, and as soon as I finished, he thanked me and said good night. I returned to my room, and while lying in bed, I tried to make sense of the day's surprising and not-so-pleasant events. Adding to my confusion was this new issue with the sunburn lotion. I sensed he was physically and sexually interested in me, but I wasn't really sure.

As future events unfolded, my gut reaction at the time had been right on, but I allowed my emotions to talk me out of acknowledging and accepting the obvious truth. Father John had been grooming and testing me for the purpose of gaining my trust. It became clear to me years later that he couldn't care less for my well-being, mental health, and emotional security; what he ultimately wanted was to sexually seduce me for his own enjoyment. As his nefarious motives became further evident, it became clearer to me that Father Raab's history was that of being a predatory priest!

July 4th Seduction

During my time as a seminarian, I maintained personal journals of my experiences. What follows is an actual journal entry I made regarding the July 4, 1979 seduction of me by Father John: *Last night, July 4th, Father John invited me to accompany him to see fireworks show outside the city limits. He said that the best view to watch was from a cemetery overlooking the river where the fireworks were to be fired overhead. I must say it was an eerie feeling walking through this cemetery with all these town people looking for places to sit and set up their folding chairs. Father John and I found a large above-ground tomb, about as big as a queen-size bed, and we sat upon it.*

The fireworks show did not last long, and sometime during the fireworks show, Father John asked me to move back and rest my back against the grave headstone. I climbed further back onto the top of the tomb, and both of us sat close together, like two people on a park bench. It was a beautiful clear summer night with a gentle cool

24

breeze blowing, and we couldn't have picked a better spot for watching the city's beautiful skyline and fireworks show. When the show was over, Father John and I remained seated, talking while all the people cleared out and went home. There was bright moonlight after the smoke cleared, which cast eerie shadows all about, and periodically I found myself looking over my shoulder at the slightest sound of something moving.

At one point when our casual conversation stopped, Father John reached over with both hands and started massaging my neck. I was picking up a particularly strong vibe that he was interested in starting something physical and was open to our "fooling around." I didn't know how to just ask him outright about this and just sat silent.

He must have sensed my apprehension and lack of response because he immediately asked me to tell him about my life before entering the seminary. I asked for him to speak first about his life before the priesthood. He told me about his family and early seminary days. I followed with brief answers about my education and the number of family members.

Again, he asked me to tell him about myself, and this time I sensed he wanted to know where I was at sexually. He sat right next to me with one leg, up against mine, and one hand pressing on my shoulder. The sex "vibe" was definitely there, and I finally came right out and asked him, "Are you physically attracted to me, or are you just an extremely 'touchy-feely' person?" He responded, "Yes, I am both." Then I asked, "Are you sexually attracted to me?" And again, he replied, "Yes."

At this point, I did not know what else to say; after all, he was an ordained priest, my superior and spiritual director, and we had both taken vows of celibacy. I was actually beginning to feel emotionally attached and physically attracted to him, and yet I also felt an urgency to get away from this situation, for both our sakes. I told him that this was a dangerous situation for us to be in and that this was very hard for me to say, "We need to get back to the rectory." He looked directly at me, smiled reassuringly, and said that he admired my honesty and that he was glad I had said it.

I felt instantly relieved to hear him confirm my response and praised God for the strength to say what I did. I definitely did not want to jeopardize this friendship by engaging in sexual play with him or just having sex for the immediate gratification of it, and I told him this. I felt so good about resisting this tremendous temptation and thanked him for accepting my comments and listening to my concerns.

We changed the subject for a moment and talked about the many beautiful bright stars out that night. I was so happy, and I wanted to thank him with an embrace for listening and respecting my words. He had moved away from sitting directly next to me, and I crawled over next to him and put my arms around him. Our embrace was long, warm, and deeply sensitive. I felt a tremendous sense of love at that moment for Father John, like I'd never felt before.

I was feeling so confident, supported, and loved by him that I completely relaxed in his arms. I no longer felt the threat of anything sexual happening. We had both, so I thought, acknowledged that our commitment to our vow of celibacy and sexual abstinence was the most loving gift we could share with each other.

At the end of the embrace, I pulled away, and he looked me directly in the eyes and briefly, very tenderly kissed me on the lips. It was a surprise and seemed genuinely respectful. He pulled back momentarily to study my reaction, then held my head in both his hands and once again leaned in and kissed me on the lips. This time the kiss was harder and more sensual. We held each other tighter, and he very sensuously began to French kiss me. His kiss was so incredibly stimulating and passionate that I was completely overwhelmed. No one had ever treated me this way or with such passion. I instantly felt myself surrendering my entire being to him and fell undeniably "head-over-heels." in love!

Father John moved up on top of me and, while kissing me, began to undo my pants. I felt his erect penis pressing against my legs through his walking shorts, which he kept on. He reached inside my pants and, while French kissing me, masturbated me until I climaxed.

My body and mind exploded in sensations I could never have imag-ined. It was tremendous! I was so overwhelmed with emotion and joy I could no longer think or speak.

After surviving years of childhood sexual abuse, incest, and phys-ical manipulations, I now thought I was finally experiencing what real, gentle, honest love must be. I was not to find out just how wrong I was until several emotionally painful and devastating months later, when my summer assignment was over, and I returned home without Father John to Los Angeles.

For the next month and a half after that July 4th night, Father John took every opportunity to see me alone. He would caress me and flirt with me, even visit me in my bedroom at night before we retired. Most times, he just hugged me, and once in a while, he kissed me on the lips. He often offered to massage my back and legs, which I admittedly enjoyed it. Father John told me how much he enjoyed us lying together, face to face, fully clothed while rubbing our erect pe-nises up against each other.

On one occasion, Father John rubbed himself up against me so much that he climaxed right in his walking shorts. I eventually came to realize that Father John believed that as long as he did not physi-cally expose himself or masturbate, he wasn't really engaging in a sexual act or breaking his celibacy vow. This, in my opinion, is how Father John justifies remaining a "celibate" priest while physically at-tracted to and sexually interested in younger men.

Father John's affectionate behavior changed dramatically to-wards me after that 4th of July seduction. He now seemed content just to want to physically arouse me with gentle hugs, tender ca-resses, and long embraces. As soon as Father John noticed I was physically aroused, he immediately stopped being affectionate, pulled away, and left the room. He seemed to enjoy getting me ex-cited than seeing me frustrated every time he left. I didn't understand why he would do this. It was cruel, extremely frustrating, and at times felt like torture.

In late August of that year, I left Father John at our parish in Fort Worth, Texas, and returned home to Los Angeles to prepare to move to Berkeley, California, to begin studies for my masters in theology. While preparing to begin my studies in LA, I received several letters from Father John. Not once did he mention our recent sexual relationship or intimate 4th of July experience, and absolutely nothing was expressed on the same level as his often proclaimed profound love for me. I couldn't understand what had changed or if I had done something to turn Father John away. His letters were now cold, formal, and completely devoid of any loving emotion. I was overwhelmed by heartache and grew increasingly grief-stricken and depressed.

I finally saw Father John once more while we were both attending an annual retreat at the Claretian Renewal Center in Los Angeles. He was preparing to leave for a mission assignment in Nigeria to supervise new young seminarians. One evening during this retreat, he invited me to meet him late that evening in his private room. I was beside myself and couldn't wait.

When I got to his door, I noticed Father John peering out from a crack in the open door watching for me. As soon as I entered, we immediately stripped out of our clothes, down to our underwear. Father John lifted me onto his bed and lay on top of me, as was his preference. As had been the case each time before, we got each other "off" by hugging and rubbing up against each other's "concealed." erections. Once again reinforcing Father John's outrageous thinking, I reasoned that it wasn't actual sex if we still kept our underwear on. Imagine that! But at the time, I did not care; I truly thought I was in love, or what my confused mind perceived to be love.

Father John never again confessed his special interest in me or expressed how wonderful I was. He had achieved his goal of seducing me and no longer felt the need to invest pleasant, caring compliments upon a "conquered" soul. Father John had successfully seduced me and had no further interest in continuing our intimate relationship. I've subsequently learned that this is typical behavior of sexual predators once they have sexually assaulted their intended prey.

That was the last time I had any physical, sexual contact with Father John. It was an extremely disappointing and heartbreaking encounter. I felt I had been used, taken advantage of, and psychologically manipulated. I left his room deeply hurt, emotionally devastated, and wanting nothing more to do with him. I experienced for myself right then and there what a selfish, insincere, and sinister human being Father John truly was and, most likely, still is.

Chapter 4

Abandonment Aftermath

Father John Raab left for the Claretian mission in Nigeria in December of 1979. I was devastated by his departure and emotionally void. He expressed no sorrow or sadness about our separation. He told me he would write and that he looked forward to our reunion sometime in the coming year. I was distraught and fell apart emotionally. I felt like the first true love of my adult life had totally abandoned me, and I was now forced to deal with my own overwhelming feelings of emptiness, sadness, and despair. I could not sleep and began having digestive problems, to the point of rectal bleeding—an ulcer, no doubt. I felt as though I had experienced a death in the family. I was miserable, and no one around me knew it. I forced myself to act normal in front of my peers, superiors, family, and co-workers.

Externally, I pretended to be the picture of emotional health. But, inside, I was seriously depressed and filled with emotional pain. I knew that by recalling the suicidal state I had experienced as a teen, I was in serious mental trouble and in need of help. I vividly recalled the hopeless state of depression I was in at 16 years of age, which led me to contemplate suicide, but I was never going to go there again. I knew that my only chance for healing was to seek immediate professional counseling.

I requested therapy and started interviewing therapists who might help me to sort through the emotional grief and figure out what had happened. Initially, I sought out "religious" counselors, but I realized that each came with their own bias with regards to faith and sexual behavior. The process of seeking out a qualified therapist, someone with who I could feel comfortable, was by no means easy. I had to go through several therapist interviews and sessions before I finally found a therapist who would be helpful. He turned out to be a non-religious, male professional therapist who specialized in issues of intimacy and human sexuality.

"Dear John" Letter

The following letter was sent to Father John after I had completed hours of intense psychotherapy. I believe it demonstrates the tremendous advances I had made as a result of attending regular therapy sessions. The letter is dated November 25, 1979. Father John had been out of my life for two months: Dear John,

Do you remember the day I said that no matter what happens in the future, no matter what trouble or difficulties you may get into because of your sexual orientation? I would love and support you no matter what? Do you remember? Well, I still will do these things; however, I have given this much thought and now want to add that I don't want to wait until something happens or until you get hurt by your particular needs. I don't want to see anything happen to you or to anyone else for that matter. Therefore, I share with you the following thoughts and feelings.

I really have to work at controlling my own sexual inclinations and desires in light of my religious commitment and especially in my ministry. The day I give up on this will be the day I have to leave the religious life. I cannot ignore this fact. I need to learn what to do and how to act when I am attracted, stimulated, and tempted by another man because if I don't do this, I could really hurt someone as well as myself. The risks are high, and the consequences are extremely dangerous, especially for a celibate religious. I'm sure you've already thought of this, but I feel that thinking about it, at this point, may not be enough.

I want to learn to live a healthy, happy, and wholesome celibate life. I want and need someone to help me arrive at this goal. I may/may not ever reach it, but I am making every possible effort towards doing so. I will not allow myself to run away, even when it hurts to face the reality of my lack of control.

I will not ignore the difficulties that I have in dealing with my sexuality and orientation. If I did this, it would mean that I would have to forfeit all of the beautiful life God has allowed me to experience within my religious life so far.

I am doing everything possible to keep what I have, and I'll be damned if my sexual orientation and actions are going to be the cause of my forfeiting what I now have. I have had to admit my own weakness and incapability of dealing constructively with my sexuality. I cannot do it alone, and I will not do it alone.

Since you left in September, I have sought professional counseling, and I have discussed our relationship with my therapist. I am deeply concerned about my future as a priest. I go twice a week, and it's been extremely helpful. It, likewise, has been extremely painful, often humiliating, and I don't usually look forward to the sessions. I keep reminding myself that it is all for my own good, that it will help me in the long run. I will at least be much clearer about myself and how I can best handle related situations. It's better that I get through this now than to be sorry later. My future as a religious, as a priest, is too important for me not to do all I can to gain a better understanding and control of my inclinations.

My immediate concern, John, is likewise for you. I'm concerned about the present and future opportunities, especially with regards to your sexual inclinations and attractions. I remember you mentioned to me once that you're constantly working on this exact situation, that you've thought and prayed a lot about it, just as I have and still do. I don't feel that this is enough.

After reflecting upon all you've shared with me about your earlier days in the seminary, the time you got accused of sexually approaching someone, up to the more recent encounter with that young convert, then to our own relationship, I can't help but feel real concern for you. From the very little I know about your experiences, John, and just looking at these, I fear that this kind of thing will happen again. I have to ask, where is your life going? What direction are you headed? Please be honest, John. I am honest with you; you mean too much to me for me not to challenge you in this way. Your priest-hood is of great importance. Am I making any sense, John? Do you understand my concern?

Can you, at this time, do everything possible to avoid any type of physical encounter with anyone? I feel a responsibility, John, that forces me to ask these questions of you. Personal, yes, but much more serious. I myself, as your dear friend, do not feel that you're fully capable of doing these things on your own.

Perhaps you've thought you can to a certain extent, but that may no longer be enough or the case. I see your situation there as having serious ramifications, John. Please keep in mind that I am speaking from experience, and I do not want to see you hurt or suffer, nor do I want to see anyone else whom you might know go through these things, either.

It is my opinion and feeling, just as it all applies to myself right now, that you are, as a person, the most important concern, not your ministry. Your ministry may suffer because of this, not the physical distance in which you find yourself. You should be the priority, John. I am referring to you getting some professional counseling.

This probably is not available to you there but is here in Los Angeles. I feel that as a priority you should consider this option and take advantage of it as soon as possible. It will not hurt or damage you in the long run. However, it may if you do nothing about it.

I hope you see my concern here, John, and more importantly, my love and support. All of what I've said so far has been very difficult for me to say, and I wish I didn't need to say these things, but that's not the case, and everything must be said. Dealing with the reality of our sexual orientation is painful, and each time we deal with it, we can be sure that there will exist an element of pain.

This fear and uncomfortableness should not stop us from healing and will not stop me either. There have been several things that have become evident to me through my therapy sessions:

1. Our particular relationship can never be what it was or ended up being—physical and sexual.

2. *For me, an exclusive physical relationship is completely out of the question and no longer an open consideration. It is contrary to my commitment as a professed religious candidate.*

It is contrary to our religious lifestyle. These two facts have become firm realities for me if I intend to remain in a celibate religious community ministering to people. I do intend to do this.

I said I am honest with you, John, so I will not hide this either. Without revealing your name, I have shared our experience, mine as well as yours, with Father Brian Doran, a close and respected friend who has been very supportive, understanding, and helpful. He is more than willing to talk about all this with you, should you ever feel you need or want to. My sincere hope is that you would be open to it.

There are too many consequences, risks, and problems involved in our future as priests, not to do or say anything about it. I really do care about our future as religious, as ministers. Both of us have much to offer. Both of us have specific skills, talents, and insights that can and do help others. Let's not waste these, John. My life and future as a priest means everything to me . . . how about you?

I have said all that I feel needs to be said at this time, John. Do not be angry or afraid; I care too much for you. You are not and will not be left alone, especially by me. I'm in the same boat, my friend. I would like to see you have a better understanding of yourself and your situation with a better means of dealing with "things." (you know what I'm talking about), things that will affect you for the rest of your life. I feel it is time that you started caring and ministering more to yourself than to anyone else right now. Speaking from my own feelings, of course! Written with much love and care, Hank…

PS Whatever it is you're feeling now, I'm still with, and for, you."

Several months passed before I heard from Father John. He wrote to me about how much he was enjoying his new overseas assignment in Nigeria with the new seminarians and made it a point to express how much he enjoyed swimming with them in the local river. I knew right away what he meant by that and felt disgusted and sick for the young seminarians involved. I truly regret that at that time, I chose not to alert anyone because of my desire not to "go there again." and to just move on with my life. Looking back on Father John's response, I see clearly now how he felt confident enough in his presumed sense of power over me to indicate in his letters his continued sexual escapades with other young seminarians. He must have known that there was nothing I would say or do about this, and at the time, he was right, and he counted on this.

I chose, right then and there, to put our relationship behind me and never again replied to any of Father John's letters. I did not permit myself to think about those Nigerian seminarians, who I believed, were being groomed and sexually assaulted by him. I just wanted to stop thinking about Father John and how upset and disturbed his memory still made me feel.

Chapter 5

Church Response

In 1995, some fifteen years after leaving the Claretian Missionary Order, I received a brief letter from Father John attempting to reestablish communication with me. I did not reply but became alarmed when Father John indicated in this note that he was seeking yet another overseas mission assignment working with young students. After several days of serious contemplation, I felt compelled to report the sexual assault I had experienced by Father John to his current religious superiors. This was the first time I ever spoke about my traumatic experience with Father John to anyone within the Claretian Missionary Order.

I sent written correspondences as warnings to the Claretian Provincial regarding Father John's predatory behavior and future assignments. I'm told that my letters are on file with the Claretian Missionary Order and their responses speak for themselves. I first sent the following letter to Father Frank Ferrante, one of the Claretian Provincial government representatives and a former House of Studies supervisor of mine. This letter was sent on January 24, 1995:

Dear Father Ferrante,

I'm writing to request your recommendation on a very personal concern of mine. The year before I left the community, I had spent a summer in Ft. Worth at Saint Anne's parish; I believe it was called. There I met Father John Raab and worked the entire summer under his influence and direction. It was also there that Father Raab seduced me into a physical, sexual relationship with him. It is my feeling

36

now that he took advantage of me and caused me great emotional and spiritual distress.

That Fall, he was sent away to Nigeria. I was devastated by the separation and could not confide in my superiors the pain I experienced. It was this experience and relationship that ultimately led to my request for a formal "Leave of Absence" from the Claretian Missionary Order.

During my absence from the Claretians, Father Raab continued to correspond with me from Nigeria, informing me how much he loved it and especially his relationship with so many seminarians. On one occasion, Father John came to visit me and brought photos of himself and the "students" bathing and swimming in a local river. He told me how much he enjoyed swimming with the students and that they would "wrestle" and hold each other a lot while swimming. There was an implication of sexual arousal between him and the students, which at the time, I gave little thought to.

I then recalled an outing that Father John, the entire Ft. Worth CMF community and I made it to a lake near San Marcos. I vividly recall Father John holding me in the water and pressing his "hard-on" up against my back. He would caress my butt and stroke my penis whenever no one was looking. He was very deceptive and cunning among the others swimming around us. No one ever saw or even suspected anything physical going on between us. This "playfulness" eventually led to sexual encounters between us back at the rectory and away from the rectory.

I have received several letters from Father John this past year informing me that he wishes to return to Nigeria. I have not answered any of his letters, nor do I wish to correspond with him. I am concerned about his being placed in a position of authority over younger males. It is my opinion that Father Raab is a sexual predator and should not be allowed to have control over younger students, especially seminarians! I was informed by Father Raab himself about several sexual affairs with younger men in Ft. Worth while he and I were involved and was even introduced to one who worked near the rectory.

As you well know, my life's work is working with adult male victims of childhood trauma and sexual victimization. I recognize the behavior; I have experienced this man's method of operation for making physical, sexual contact with other males. I have a moral obligation to speak of what I know about this perpetrator.

I want this information to be given to those who would assign Father John to a teaching or spiritual director position among students. Please advise me how I can pass on this information and to whom it needs to be addressed. I will hold off sending a more detailed letter of this to your current Provincial Superior until I hear from you first. I trust you understand my position and urgency in this. I look forward to your response.

Sincerely,

Hank Estrada

P.S. Obviously, Father Raab has no idea that I'm writing this as a result of his recent letters to me and so I would welcome your recommendation as to who in the order should be the one to inform him of the contents of this letter.

I received a reply from Father Ferrante dated January 26, 1995. The actual letter is shown on the following page. Per Fr. Ferrante's recommendation, here is the letter I sent to Claretian Provincial Fr. John Martens on January 29, 1995:

Dear Father Martens,

Enclosed find a letter I recently sent to Father Ferrante. He suggested I send you this copy. The letter is self-explanatory in its intent and importance. Although fourteen or so years have passed since I was a seminarian, I feel the enclosed information is critical to the future ministerial assignment of Father John Raab. Feel free to discuss this matter with Father Ferrante. If you feel it necessary, you may reference me and my letter as the informative source to Father Raab. Please understand that I wish to avoid confronting Father Raab regarding this and am not open to any further direct communication between Father Raab and myself.

If I can provide you with any further information regarding this issue, please don't hesitate to contact me. Thank you in advance for your understanding and assistance. On February 6, 1995, Provincial Father Martens sent the following response.

CLARETIAN RENEWAL CENTER

CM|F

Hank Estrada   January 26, 1995
P.O. Box 6545
Santa Fe, New Mexico 87502-6545

Dear Hank,

    Today I received your January 24th letter. I appreciate your concern and definitely would recommend that the contents of the letter be brought to the attention of the present provincial, namely, Fr. John Martens, C.M.F., whose address is below.
    I tried calling you a couple of times but there was no answer. I hope to talk with you soon by phone-- we did not have much time to converse when we by chance ran into each other at the Mervyn's parking lot during the Christmas season.
    Hank, my prayers are with you. Thanks for taking the time to share with me what I understand to be a very important concern of yours.

                                    Sincerely,

                                    Frank

                                    Frank Ferrante, C.M.F.

1119 WESTCHESTER PLACE, LOS ANGELES, CA 90019   (213) 737-8464

CLARETIAN MISSIONARIES

February 6, 1995

Mr. Hank Estrada
P.O. Box 6545
Sante Fe, NM 87502-6545

Dear Mr. Estrada:

Thank you for your letter dated January 29, 1995. It was expedient for me to know the information you sent me concerning Fr. John Raab. I would appreciate it if you would send me a copy of the letters you received from John Raab, if you still have them. I also would like to know, if possible, the seasonal time of the year and the year when physical sexual behavior took place.

I want to thank you again for sharing this information with me. I want to assure you that we are conducting a thorough investigation into this matter. It is our policy to do all that we can to prevent evil behavioral conduct from happening.

My prayers are with you, and may the Lord help you in your healing process.

Sincerely in Jesus with Mary,

Fr. John Martens, C.M.F.
Provincial Superior

THE CONGREGATION OF SONS OF THE IMMACULATE HEART OF MARY OF THE WESTERN PROVINCE, INC.
1119 WESTCHESTER PLACE, LOS ANGELES, CALIFORNIA 90019

I immediately wrote back, saying I did not save Father Raab's letter but did provide him with the exact dates of my experience. I never heard anything further from Provincial Martens or the administrator Father Ferrante regarding the actions they supposedly took regarding Father John. To this day, I have no idea if anything was done with or for Father John, including sending him to an appropriate therapist or rehabilitation program. I assume that given the church's pattern of conscious denial—nothing was done.

I continued working with a therapist and eventually came to the conclusion that Father John was a sexual predator who, when he was my assigned superior took advantage of his authority and who's ultimate goal was to pursue physical contact between us.

CHAPTER 6

MEA CULPA

I came to discover during therapy that I needed to know if I could ever again experience the same level of intimacy in a one-on-one love relationship. Despite months of emotionally intense counseling, I found myself aching for the physical and emotional intimacy I experienced with Father John. I wanted to feel the same physical and emotional high and proceeded to target fellow classmates and other seminarians.

I found myself behaving as Father John had by setting up seduction scenarios. I focused special attention on certain male friends with whom I had established close, trusting ties. I'd voice compliments, perform special acts of kindness, offer assistance, and at any given opportunity offer an occasional gentle touch on the back, arms, or shoulder.

My actions were always accepted as innocent and genuine and never suspect. I found myself desperately seeking intense feelings of love and physical intimacy, and before I realized it, was headed down a now-familiar, painful road that resulted in the death of my desire to become a Catholic priest.

As an adult survivor of child sexual abuse and have experienced emotionally intense episodes of seduction and pleasure with Father John, I had a mindset that led me on two different occasions to seduce two fellow seminarians in much the same way that Father John had done to me.

I believe this strong desire to experience the same power level of intimacy that I had with Father John was behind the following two seductions. At the time, I was at a loss for words to describe what I needed or wanted emotionally and physically. These two incidents were never premeditated but occurred when circumstances provided me with the opportunity for complete privacy in a one-on-one setting.

Adam

Adam and I were roommates in the seminary. He was a year or so younger than me, and we were very close friends. Over the course of a few years of studies together, sharing a room and living in the same house, Adam and I talked openly about our personal lives, including each being gay and attracted to certain types of men. Neither of us thought of the other in a sexual or romantic way, especially because we were both striving to maintain our celibacy vows. Adam and I often talked intimately about being gay and living as celibate ordained men. We discussed our mutual frustration with trying to overcome masturbation and offered frequent support to each other when we failed. Adam shared with me that, up to this point in his adult life, he had never had a sexual experience with another man. I felt honored by his honesty and trust and sincerely loved him as a friend. I, on the other hand, and do not understand why I never shared with Adam about the sexual history between Father John and me.

Four months after Father John left, Adam and I went on an overnight trip together. It was a badly needed opportunity to get away from the hectic schedule and pressure of our academic studies and ministry assignments. The destination was a few hours away, and we enjoyed the drive immensely. We booked a room at a typically small budget hotel and, after treating ourselves to a nice dinner, watched TV and drank some wine. I'm sure that over the years, at one time or another, we were sexually curious about the other but never shared this openly.

When it was time to get into our separate beds, I wanted to show Adam how much I cared for him and asked if I could lie beside him in his bed. Adam hesitated, even said no, but I persisted by saying that all I wanted was to lie down with him, that I didn't want to get sexual.

Adam said, "I don't think I could be that close to you without wanting sex, myself." I said I understood, but my sexual urge was driving me to continue challenging his honesty.

After some silence, I again asked if he would simply allow me to just hold him. Adam let out a sigh and immediately jumped out of his bed, came over, and sat on my bed. Adam said he couldn't just lie with me and do nothing, that it would be too tempting to want to do more. Then he began frantically rubbing his hands over my chest and arms, saying over and over that he just couldn't control his sexual attraction. His eyes seemed to glaze with excitement as he increased his hand rubbing all over my body, including my crotch. He seemed obsessed with touching, rubbing, and exploring my body, quickly and erratically. After all, this was his "first" time being this close to a man, especially someone like me with whom he actually shared years of loyal friendship.

His burst of exaggerated excitement caused me concern because it wasn't like him to be so crazed and jumpy. I told him that sex was not what I was feeling, but he continued to explore my body with his eyes and hands. After a few minutes of this, Adam sensed I was not responding to him and stopped.

We were able to talk calmly with each other about what we were and were not feeling right then, how we felt about our friendship, and our religious vow of celibacy. Adam collected his thoughts and returned to his own bed. After some minutes of silence, it became obvious that he had fallen asleep.

As I lay there thinking about what had just happened, I began to feel sexually excited and thought about what the outcome would have been if I had not stopped his advances and allowed him to continue. My thoughts were becoming too much to ignore, so I decided to wake him from his sleep and talk about it. "I still want to lie next to you," I said. He sternly replied, "No, I've prayed about it and asked God for strength to overcome the temptation. I don't want anything to happen between us that I might regret."

I persisted with my desire to just lie down with him until he finally said, "Okay." I removed my briefs but left my t-shirt on. I could feel

44

his body tense up and start to tremble as I slid next to him. He whispered, "Let's not do this; we can't do this." My hands were exploring his entire body all the while he kept repeating, "We shouldn't be doing this." He then became instantly erect and gave in to the moment. We rubbed up against each other's bodies as our arms wrapped tightly around the other. I wanted to kiss him, but he said no, that he wasn't ready for it. Eventually, both of us reached climax just by holding and rubbing up against one another.

After we rinsed and washed ourselves off, we returned to our separate beds and talked a little about what had just happened. Adam said that he felt he never wanted to do that again with any man. He said he was personally disappointed in himself and overcome with guilt. I, on the other hand, felt content and satisfied knowing that we had shared something "very special." What that special something really was, was that same old, compulsive, negative sexual behavior pattern I learned as a child. I was performing a sexual act and allowing "the act" to replace intimacy, and further, any hint of emotional attachment and responsibility. I was very confused and did not know any better. And in my mind, even with all his expressed hesitancy, I thought that Adam and I were now even closer than before. Of course, this was a total misrepresentation of reality, but that is how I was "taught" to view my sexuality.

Adam grew really quiet and was visibly unhappy with himself and with me. In the end, I apologized to Adam for mentally pressuring him to engage in a sexual act despite his initial objections. I should have respected Adam for his honesty and left him alone. This scenario between Adam and I was exactly what had transpired some time before, between Father John and me. In time, I realized that I was now playing the role of the aggressor — the role of Father John — and Adam was in the role of playing myself. I was acting out the same negative pattern of using "sex as power" over another. But now, I was reversing the roles. Adam tried to talk me out of a bad situation, and I ended up persuading him to give in to my sexual drive. We never spoke about this again, and I am left to wonder if Adam, too, ever found himself repeating this with someone else.

Tate

The second time I took on the role of a sexual aggressor was in April 1980, after I had left and been away from the seminary for just a few weeks. Five former co-workers and I took a flight north to Sacramento, California, to attend a national conference. Among the group was a very handsome, young seminarian named Tate, not from my former religious community but a seminarian nonetheless. Tate and I often worked together on various religious education projects and programs. Tate was one year younger than I, extremely attractive, athletic, charming, and very sexy. Female associates and parishioners would all swoon around him whenever he entered a room. He was a very private, reserved person with a witty sense of humor. I had always been attracted to Tate and, over the years, often fantasized about being physical and having sexual contact with him.

This particular weekend, Tate and I were assigned our own private rooms with baths, directly across the hall from each other. That day was hot as we arrived at the conference facility. Walking about the facility, Tate and I came upon a large outdoor swimming pool. A tall six-foot fence surrounded the pool, and locks were on all the gates. After we had unpacked our things, Tate and I decided to climb the fence and cool off in the pool. All the other conference participants were unpacking and resting in their rooms before the conference opening session later that evening. Tate and I were the only ones in this enormous, cool, Olympic-size pool.

I had not packed swimming trunks that weekend, only a pair of walking shorts. I didn't want to get the only walking shorts I had wet, so I took my shorts and briefs off and jumped in nude; after all, the pool area was private and secure. I was neither embarrassed nor concerned. As for Tate, he had packed his swim trunks and already had them on.

Tate and I had never shared much personal information with one another outside our work environment. We knew little about each other's family background and even less regarding our sexual orientation. I always thought Tate was an extremely desirable man, and assumed he was heterosexual, and kept my personal attraction to

Tate a strict secret. We were working associates and rarely found ourselves together in a non-work-related social setting.

After I removed my clothes and dove headfirst into the pool, Tate seemed pretty surprised and even said something to the effect of "Gee, you're really brave." I could feel Tate curiously watching me as I swam around the pool in the nude. As I began swimming laps, Tate swam over and joined me. We raced a few times, back and forth; then Tate decided to remove his trunks too. Tate made a comment after swimming laps in the nude about how much easier it felt to move in the water without swimming trunks.

There was a water hose lying nearby, and we started to horseplay by spraying each other and trying to dunk the other's head underwater and eventually ending in a game of tag. After about twenty minutes of play, we both agreed to get out and lie in the sun next to the pool. Tate was a muscular, blue-eyed blond who enjoyed having a wonderful tan and took every opportunity to get one. We sunbathed upon the hot cement and casually conversed about the upcoming conference.

As we were lying on our backs, side by side, I could sense Tate trying to get a better look at me, and, of course, I was trying to do the same of him. Tate had a firm, muscular body, and I was really enjoying being nude outdoors with him. I made it a point to keep the situation as casual as possible as we lay next to each other, hoping to make him feel more comfortable. At one point, he confessed to me that he had never laid out naked before with another person. I noticed a few moments after saying this, as our conversation stumbled onto a sexual topic, that Tate began to get an erection.

Becoming conscious and uncomfortable with this, he quickly turned over onto his stomach. With that simple and sudden display, my curiosity was aroused, and my thoughts turned to perhaps getting intimate with Tate sometime during the conference. In my confused mind, his innocent display indicated an all-out opportunity.

We noticed that the time for us to prepare for the conference's evening opening session was near at hand. Tate suggested we use the adjoining shower room by the pool to give us a few minutes of extra time. We found ourselves alone in the shower room, standing side by side in adjoining stalls as we showered. I lathered up my head with shampoo, and when he mentioned that he had none, I walked over to Tate, gathered suds from the top of my head, and gently placed them on top of his.

We stood facing each other, and I began rubbing the suds through his hair for a few seconds. Tate was stunned and simply stood there grinning as the water and suds ran off his head and body. It was one of the most spontaneous and sensuous moments of my life, and I will never forget it. As a young gay man, I had only fleeting fantasies about something as sensual as this ever happening to me in real life. And yet, here I was. Tate seemed really relaxed and shut his eyes while I massaged his head with lathery suds. I let go of his head, stepped away, and waited.

When Tate opened his eyes to look at me, I smiled, then walked back over to my own shower to rinse off and got out. He told me later that he was impressed at how relaxed and confident I seemed, standing naked face-to-face with another man under those circumstances. I know he was referring to my not being instantly aroused or having an erection.

After the opening conference session and reception, I decided to retire early to my room. By the time I arrived at my room, about 9 p.m., I was consumed with thoughts of seducing Tate. I kept peering out my bedroom door, waiting for Tate to come to his room, directly across from mine. My mind raced with anticipation and excitement at the prospect of having sexual contact with Tate. As Tate walked around the corner, my heart was pounding, and I pretended to be looking for something in the corridor. "What are you doing up?" Tate asked. "I thought you were going to bed early."

He walked over and stood in my doorway as I proceeded to explain how I couldn't sleep. After a long silent pause and lots of direct lingering eye-to-eye contact, Tate said, "Well, if you still can't sleep, let me know." He stood awkwardly in the doorway for a moment, then said good night and slipped into his own room.

I paced for another hour, wondering if I should go over or just go to sleep. I secretly walked up to Tate's bedroom door and pressed my ear against the cold wood to listen for movement. My body ached to hold him, feel him, and make out with him while my conscience struggled. It was about 11 p.m. when I decided to go into Tate's room. The lights were off, and the door was unlocked, so I quietly walked in.

I turned on a small nightlight, and Tate seemed to be expecting me. I knelt down by the side of his bed and very nervously said, "I may be wrong, but do you want to sleep with me?" He blushed a little and replied, "Oh no, I was just kidding," referring to some of the sexual teasings between us earlier that day by the pool. Then Tate stopped for a moment, sat up in bed, and asked me, "Do you want to?" I said that I was open to it. He nodded OK, then threw the covers off and stood up. We walked across the hall back over to my room.

In anticipation of being successful, I had already pushed the two twin beds in the room together, hoping Tate would be open to something more happening between us. I left a small closet light on in the distance so we could still see each other. We stripped our clothes off and climbed into each other's arms. With our eyes, hands, and erections, we explored each other's bodies. His hands moved all over mine: my back, chest, arms, legs, and penis. We took turns admiring and feeling one another, and neither could believe this was happening. After a few intense moments of pleasure, we climaxed together in silence. Then Tate immediately got up, left my room, and returned to his own bed.

The next day, during the conference, I sensed Tate's subtle avoidance of me. So later that afternoon, when there was a conference break, I asked him to take a walk with me. He started the conversation by apologizing for his "horniness." I quickly stopped him by saying that I had enjoyed it and an open invitation for later that evening was his. He just answered, "Oh." He did not return the next evening, and we never spoke about it again. I can only assume that Tate also experienced personal disappointment and guilt about giving into sex as Adam had. Long after the conference was over, I learned from

49

Tate that he, too, had often fantasized about a sexual encounter with me as well.

As time progressed, I became much more confident and aggressive with directly asking individuals I was attracted to if they'd be interested in having sex with me. At the same time, I knew that this type of intimacy was not at all what I was really searching for. I was searching haphazardly for true, personal intimacy—the sharing of intense mutual feelings, thoughts, and ultimately love in its basic form—but after my disappointing encounter with Father John, these types of brief, empty sexual encounters were all I knew and focused on.

Holy Week Hustler

Living in an all-male seminary often made for a sexually stressful environment, as I physically ached for the touch of another. I found myself many times wanting to be with someone, someone to hold and become intimate with. Instead of turning to my spiritual directors for support, I would fantasize about sex with others, which lead to masturbation. Afterward, I would seek absolution and forgiveness from a senior priest in the community. Eventually, even masturbating wasn't enough to curb the stress I dealt with, and I started to consider seeking out a stranger for anonymous sex.

The first place I thought about was an adult bookstore in Hollywood, which I had driven by. The second consideration was driving to a known section of Hollywood where men walk the streets seeking "rides," but in truth, were male prostitutes, also known as hustlers. I thought that a male hustler would be a good possibility because for him, it was simply a job he would perform, and nothing more would be expected from me, aside from the exchange of money. No commitment, no getting to- know-you, no personal information sharing, just quick sex. Back then, "hot sex" for me was having oral sex performed on me or someone masturbating me to climax. My knowledge and experience of sex as a child were simplistically raw and only limited to these two specific acts. Consequently, my sexual experiences during seminary, including those with Father John, remained similar and devoid of true affection and intimacy.

One particular spring evening at the seminary, I was feeling unusually lonely and stressed and made the decision to approach a male hustler for sex. I had no idea of what I was supposed to do or how I was to go about it. All I knew was that an overwhelming sense of sexual desire drove me to seek out relief. I rationalized to myself that this was the safer alternative to getting physical with another fellow seminarian, or even worse. What follows is another journal account entry I made about this experience:

"Good Friday" on Tuesday and Wednesday of this Holy Week, I went on a silent retreat at a Franciscan retreat house in Malibu. It was very good, and the time was spent prayerfully. On Thursday morning, I returned home, and in the evening, I attended Holy Thursday liturgy. From Tuesday to Thursday, I was feeling happy and comfortable with what I had been doing, praying, sharing, contemplating, etc. I began to think about sex Thursday night after the liturgy and prayed that nothing would happen. All-day on Good Friday, I was consumed with thoughts of sex. I wanted to be reflecting on the passion of Christ prayerfully and sincerely. I found myself forcing "spiritual" thoughts and praying fervently.

I spent some of that Good Friday afternoon up in Griffith Park with a friend at the Bird Sanctuary. It is really beautiful.

There are lots of trees, evergreen shrubs, a flowing stream, dirt paths, and birds singing all around, an excellent place for prayer and contemplation. However, all I could concentrate on was every physically attractive man who passed us. When I returned home that afternoon, my mind was swimming with thoughts of sex and "getting off."

I was so sexually wound up that I snuck out of the seminary later that evening and drove up to Hollywood with the intention of picking up a male hustler. All I knew is the area where these hustlers hung out, and that was it. It never occurred to me what I would do or say once I got there, but there I went.

I have never picked up even a hitchhiker in my life because I never had the courage. This night, I had more than courage; I was sexually driven and obsessed. I drove all around the area where the male hustlers gathered, but no one would approach my car. After a while, the street was empty, and I still hadn't picked up anyone. I decided to head for the nearest adult bookstore a few blocks away. I sat parked outside, waiting for someone to pass or approach, but no one did. I was so horny and anxious to get with someone and after two hours sitting outside in my car, I decided to head home.

As I was pulling away from the curb, already resigned that nothing was going to happen, I spotted a man standing on the corner. He was looking at another man passing in a car, but the car just kept driving. I drove slowly over to the man on the corner and, with the passenger side window rolled halfway down, asked if he needed a ride. He said, "Yes," and got into my car.

I was surprised when he extended his hand, politely introduced himself, and asked what my name was. I gave him a false name and immediately asked if he lived nearby and wanted to go back to his house. I was ready to have sex and couldn't wait to make it happen. He cautiously answered, "Yes," but first, he wanted just to talk and get to know a little something about me.

He suggested we just drive around, so I did. What happened next was completely unexpected.

As I drove and he talked, I found him to be engaging, bright, friendly, sincere, and interesting. I started to see him as a human being, a nice person and stopped focusing on just having sex with him. During the conversation, I lost the intense desire for sex and found myself feeling very sad for him, for how he was hustling himself out and using his body for sex with strangers to make money. I asked him if he was happy and tired of this way of living. He abruptly asked me not to ask him about that and wanted to be let out of the car. I had obviously hit a sensitive nerve with him but was compelled to learn more and possibly help him. He wanted nothing of it and started to resent personal inquiries of his hustling lifestyle. I told him that he was the first man I had ever picked up and that after learning about him, I no longer saw him as just someone for sex. I had changed my mind and now had only sympathy and compassion for him. Sex was definitely out of the question for me at that point. He asked me not to lay "that trip" on him and quickly changed the subject.

After driving a little more and talking, he quickly moved in closer next to me, took my hand in his, and held it. He looked me directly in the eyes and waited for me to make a sexual advance. I was unable to move and could just barely muster up the words, "I can't do it." I now saw this guy in a completely different, non-sexual light. He knew I was serious and asked if

he should get out of the car right there. I told him I would drop him off where I picked him up. While I was driving away, I saw him walk up to another single dark figure seated inside a parked car and climb in. The car slowly drove away, turned left into an alley, parked, and shut off all its lights.

As I headed back to the seminary, I felt a surge of mixed emotions and thoughts. I felt happy and hopeful that I had not acted out sexually with him. I was enlightened by this man's brief conversation but realized that there is always so much more than just achieving a physical, sexual climax.

The next day, Saturday, and right up to Easter Sunday, I was feeling fairly stoic, not particularly excited or depressed. It was a typical solemn Easter Sunday until that evening while watching the conclusion of the miniseries Jesus of Nazareth. I was really identifying with the character of Peter and was especially moved when Jesus told Peter that he would deny ever knowing him. Peter answered, "No, Lord! I love you . . . I will give my life for you!" Then shortly thereafter, Peter denies knowing Jesus and watches his crucifixion.

I felt like Peter denying Jesus when I went out on Good Friday evening and was thinking only of myself. I had experienced giving into ignoring my faith, turning my back on my belief in Christ, and still seeking to fulfill my sexual desires. I was wrong for how far I let myself go that Good Friday, yet I knew I was forgiven.

This overwhelming sense of forgiveness hit me as I was watching the conclusion of the Jesus of Nazareth movie. The scene is Jesus, after the resurrection, seated with his arms around John and Peter,

53

telling them he must go. Peter sadly says, "Don't leave us. The night is long." Then Peter rests his head gently on Jesus's chest. Jesus, holding Peter close, says, "I go now to the Father, but know this, there is an immediate extreme close up of Jesus' face and piercing eyes as he says, "I am with you always, even until the end of the world." At that moment, Jesus was not only looking at me but was directly speaking to me about where I had just come from.

I broke down in uncontrollable tears and cried so deeply that I could not catch my breath. I felt totally forgiven and loved in spite of my selfish behavior that Good Friday night. I went to bed with an in-spiring sense of God's love for me and a tremendous sense of for-giveness for giving in to sexual temptations.

That particular Easter remains one of the most significant spiritual experiences in my seminary training. Over the years, both then and now, I would successfully learn to confront sexual distractions while at other times just struggle through them.

CHAPTER 7

INCEST HISTORY

You must be wondering by now what happened in my childhood that made me susceptible as an adult to reoccurring incidents of victimization. These answers are evident in the following recount of a few significant moments in my childhood.

I was the oldest child of five children. My mother was a homemaker, and my father was a deliveryman for a national beer company. We lived in a small three-bedroom house in East Los Angeles: one room shared by my two brothers and me, another room for my sister, and the master bedroom. Dad had an older brother, Oscar, whom Dad claimed was mentally disabled due to a childhood accident. Uncle Oscar lived with us for most of my childhood, sometimes sleeping on the sofa in the living room and sometimes with me. My Dad worked very hard and enjoyed numerous beers after work and on weekends.

My father rarely shared any information about his own childhood and, as I reflect back, he was quite secretive with anything having to do with his own adolescent years. I came to understand that he himself carried significant scars from childhood that contributed to his alcoholism, violent arguments, and physical attacks against my mother and me.

"Dad and me."

In 1985, after 25 years of maintaining my secret about being sexually abused by my uncle Oscar and after convincing myself that I was his only victim; I sadly discovered that a nephew of mine had also been victimized by this uncle. I was told that one of my nephews, about 11 years old, was abruptly and without reason beginning to behave poorly at school and having difficulties concentrating in class. My instinct "clicked," and I instantly knew that Uncle Oscar probably has something to do with this because I was aware that he often volunteered to babysit this particular nephew. By remaining silent all those years, I had inadvertently protected Uncle Oscar and allowed him the opportunity to claim yet another child victim.

I became extremely angry and upset by this horrific revelation and decided that I now had to tell my family about my long-held secret—my own sexual experiences with this abusive uncle. I felt a tremendous amount of guilt and rage for not having said anything about Uncle Oscar, but I knew he had to be confronted.

My first concern was to convince my nephew of his innocence in the incident. This conversation was one of the most difficult I have ever had, especially with a young nephew. As gently as I could, I told my nephew about my own history with this uncle, about being uncomfortably touched by him, and most importantly, asked if anything similar had ever happened to him. He dropped his head in shame, nodded, and whispered, "yes." I felt satisfied that he had admitted this to me, but I was also angered by the confirmation. I told my nephew that I was sorry that he, too, had been molested. I promised him that I would always be available for him if he ever wanted to talk more about it. I suggested he consider talking with a professional counselor, but it was clear to me that he was uncomfortable and declined. I felt responsible for his victimization and upset with myself for never saying anything about being sexually molested by Uncle Oscar. Uncle Oscar had used every subtle, predatory tactic to molest me, and now my nephew, showering us both with special favors, money, and gifts while praising us with compliments and sincere professions of his love.

After talking with my nephew, I approached the other members of my immediate family individually. Denial, shock, doubt, anger, and resentment best describe their reactions. I met with my parents first and told them that I had been sexually molested for years by Uncle Oscar. Mom said nothing, and Dad simply hung his head and stopped looking at me. It was as if he knew all along but had hoped it would not happen.

When I pressed them for a response, Dad looked me in the eyes and said, "What do you want me to do? He's my brother." I was shocked and deeply hurt when I heard his words. I will never forget that moment, his exact words together with the pathetic look on his face. Any feelings of love that a son could have for his father died in that instant and have never returned. Despite all the violent attacks by my father against me, this had to be the absolute worst thing he had ever done. The words he spoke inflicted more pain than any physical punches and slapped face I had ever endured. After noticing my shocked reaction, he said, "Do what you have to do," which I took to mean, "Go to the authorities." I don't remember either parent saying they were sorry this had happened, or asking how I was doing, or even if I wanted their help. I didn't receive so much as an extended hand of support from either of them. All I remember is my dad's unbelievably cold response: "What do you want me to do? He's my brother."

I sat before them, feeling completely unloved, unsupported, and insignificant. I didn't know these two empty souls, these strange people sitting before me—my parents. I kept asking myself if they had really just ignored all the childhood years I spent in a terrible household of secret denial, suffering at the hands of a sexual predator? Had they really meant to abandon and cast me off, an innocent child now grown and forced to fend for myself? Were they really so overcome with my news that they became mute when faced with their own son's history? I was shocked but remained calm and in control of the devastating feelings churning within me. Much of what transpired between us that afternoon is now difficult for me to recall. But I do remember the brief, personal talk I had with my nephew, and if that is all the positive gratitude, I am given to remember, then so be it.

As far as I'm aware, my nephew never received counseling for the abuse perpetrated upon him. All I know is that while in his early teens, he got his girlfriend pregnant. As I know today, this behavior can be a typical response of a male survivor who does not get professional counseling and feels the misdirected need to prove his masculinity by fathering children. Today, my nephew lives with children of his own and a wife and is admirably attempting to take on the breadwinning role of making a living for his family. We never again spoke of the incident, nor have we spoken to each other since that day. I wished healing and peace of mind for him, but I know from experience that, even with therapy, this secret of abuse most certainly haunts him still.

My sister and I considered filing a police report but the statues of limitations had expired for me, and since my nephew did not want to pursue legal action, there was nothing more we could do at the time. Uncle Oscar was simply sent to live with another brother and our family never again spoke of this situation.

As far as I know, Uncle Oscar never received professional therapy for his pedophilia, nor has anyone else ever confronted him. For years, Uncle Oscar remained and was known as "the uncle you don't ever want to leave your children alone with," and yet, even with this weak acknowledgment, relatives to this day refuse to discuss why.

Typical family outing, Uncle Oscar (far right) in white shirt.

Unfortunately, my sister, nephew, and family members simply choose to ignore the topic. Despite my coming forward as a former victim of Uncle Oscar, the authorities could do nothing without the cooperation of those family members who were directly impacted. This personal disclosure has been beset with difficulties and controversy. I became the unnamed "whistle-blower." Although most in my extended family were aware of the abuse, no one ever spoke of it openly. I remained an outcast by some family members, a villain in their eyes for talking publicly about this family secret, for actually having the gall to bring it out into the open. I was re-victimized, looked upon as though I were both the perpetrator and the offender!

Sadly, many family members still choose to deny the truth, the possibility that within their household, childhood molestation might be taking place. They do this by ignoring the brave disclosures of survivors of this abuse. To this day, not one specific action has been taken by my immediate family to get psychological assistance or treatment for Uncle Oscar. I'm sure there must have been other victims since my own abuse, but they remain silent, dwelling in personal shame and fears of their own. It is my hope that perhaps now, after reading these personal pages, other survivors might gain the courage to also come forward and speak out.

I am aware that Uncle Oscar lived to be in his mid-80s and no doubt victimized others in his care. Unfortunately, those around him grasped the easy choice of remaining silent, even proudly defending his perverse actions despite being confronted with the undeniable facts. More ironically, Uncle Oscar was further protected by by-laws that require that perpetrators be caught "in the act of committing" the sexual assault versus past history of abuse and public testimony. So, as things unfolded, he remained a protected predator to the end.

Who Will Protect Me?

My father rarely spent time with my four siblings or me, and in those rare moments when he was physically present, he was psychologically numb and detached. A beer not far from his grasp, alcohol was his favorite companion. It was during times like these that he would severely reprimand and discipline us for what he perceived to be our childlike behavior and would constantly and sternly order us to do simple yet unimportant tasks, just for the sake of displaying his authority. He also made it perfectly clear that he wanted us, kids, to leave him alone each night after he arrived home from work.

At the end of a typical workday, he'd arrive home just after dark, kiss Mom hello, remove his boots and work jacket, toss them near his chair, and head to the refrigerator for his "first" beer to relax. Being innocent children, we would follow him to his favorite olive green recliner and ask if he brought us anything. This was followed by a labored, strained sigh of relief and by the phrase, "Boy, I'm tired."

There were times he would briefly ask how we were doing, then, without waiting for our reply, he would pick up the evening newspaper and begin to read. By his lack of interest and mental detachment, he made it very clear to us that after he had arrived home from work, we were not to "complicate his life" with our "concerns." He just didn't want to be bothered with us.

It was understood that for the rest of the evening, we were expected to stay away and not talk to him unless he spoke first. The only attention we would be offered was when he'd address one of us with a request for another beer. Mom's routine would begin by putting supper on the table as the children patiently waited in the living room, entertaining themselves by watching TV. When it came time to eat, Dad often directed Mom to serve the kids and herself, and always add: "I'll eat later."

At the end of dinner and after Mom had cleaned the kitchen of dishes, Dad would finally decide he wanted to eat. He'd instruct her to serve him his dinner. She had to leave whatever task she was in the middle of doing and, at his convenience, reheat his entire meal. This was basically the evening's routine for most days of the week. Even with a child's limited comprehension, I was able to see that this situation was terribly wrong. I felt deeply pained for my mom because watching her having to do so much work, with the added task of jumping to my father's orders, only meant more work for her. But Dad never seemed to care, and he never offered to assist her with a single thing. Four or five beers later, Dad would often start an argument with Mom over something that never made any sense. It was, and seemed, just for the sake of arguing.

Family portrait, I'm in a white shirt (top left), age 14.

I remember at one of these times, and Mom got so upset when Dad wanted to be fed two hours after dinnertime that she served it lukewarm. Dad was furious and threw the plate full of food into the sink and shouted obscenities at Mom, threatening to teach her a lesson and demanding she shows more respect for him.

Dad had a violent temper and always took his personal inadequacies and job-related frustrations out on Mom. As a child, I remember constantly trying to distract him with play or by asking a question or by making a statement about something totally unrelated, just to divert him away from Mom. Sometimes it worked; most times, it didn't. And as I got older, he began to turn his alcoholic rage on me.

In contrast to Dad, Uncle Oscar would take me to the park and push me on the swings. He would always tell me how special I was and how much he loved me. He'd treat me to many of the things I enjoyed, such as being towed in my favorite red wagon. He would do things for me that my father did not care to do or be bothered with doing. If I wanted anything, Uncle Oscar would promise to get it for me. And he would remind me over and over that, I was his "special" nephew. Given this status, and despite his constant sexualized touching, I felt in my own childlike mind that I could not betray his affection without risking the loss of the many treats and his ever-ready attentions. I sought simply to feel love, wanted, and validated.

When I was a little boy, Uncle Oscar would silence me into submission with promises of ice cream, candy, and toys. Understand that my Uncle Oscar was the exact opposite of my father in his caring demeanor and attention. Uncle Oscar always presented himself as being patient, gentle, supportive, and affectionate—qualities which my father seldom revealed to me, if ever.

I ended up protecting my uncle, and thereby, protecting the only refuge of love that I knew. As a child, I found myself in a very difficult position: either to keep quiet about the sexual touching that was taking place between us or to tell my parents and destroy this special relationship with my uncle. I was afraid of getting Uncle Oscar and myself into trouble. I was also afraid that if my parents were to find out about us, they would no longer want me and would abandon me.

I was especially afraid of my father's violent temper and that he would hurt Uncle Oscar if he ever found out. I was afraid and completely terrified.

Dad and Uncle Oscar were both alcoholics, and periodically, dad would get into violent arguments with mom, physically assault her, and later as I grew older, assault me. I lived in constant fear that he would seriously hurt my mother and Uncle Oscar if he ever learned of the sexual molestations happening right under his own roof. I loved Uncle Oscar and always looked forward to his positive praises, gifts, and supportive attention and would be devastated if they were to end.

Unfortunately, as a child, I did not send out clues or indicate that I was sexually abused, at least not consciously. Uncle Oscar and I had a very "special relationship," a "secret" that no one else on earth knew, and I wasn't about to tell.

The remainder of our sexual relationship lasted until I was 16. By then, being an adolescent, I learned to manipulate Uncle Oscar into engaging in sex only when I wanted. As a developing adolescent boy, I admit that, although the physical pleasures of sexual contact were heightened and intensified, I still felt tremendous guilt and shame for the sex that was taking place between us. Depression instantly followed every orgasm that occurred, and self-loathing quickly set in. It was not right, and I knew it.

Alcoholism in my family played a large part in my not being able to confidently open up and communicate my experiences to my parents. My father was unapproachable because of his continuous substance abuse. My mother tried desperately to keep the wholesome family charade going, a clean face of normality, and she was willing to accomplish this even if it meant ignoring the abusive environment within which her helpless children were being raised. Apparently, everyone in the family knew that there was "something" different about Uncle Oscar, something that was never talked about but silently understood. And yet, each of my parents' brothers and sisters would consistently hand their children over to Uncle Oscar to babysit while they attended family functions and social events.

I was aware of this unspoken rule even at a very young age. I understood not to talk badly about family-related issues because Dad would get upset. My parents, like many at the time, were often pre-occupied with paying bills, keeping a job, and providing a home for all of us. This was made very clear as financial issues were the source of many an argument between my parents. So how could I ever approach them with my questions or concerns? They had too many of their own.

Dad and me (front right) surrounded by Dad's brothers. Uncle Oscar holds baby sister and beer can (left).

Additionally, I was psychologically burdened by the thought that my existence was a large source of my father's annoyance and irri-tations. So much pressure, stress, and tension existed in my family that my reaction was to hold everything inside me. I felt it was useless to wish and pray for my abuse and other family problems to go away. Nothing stopped the terrors of my father's rage or answered my ques-tions about why I wasn't able to make Dad happy to see me or want to spend time with me like Uncle Oscar always did.

Today I am aware that my abuse experienced as a child is not at all unique or isolated. I chose to share these personal experiences with you in order to describe, in a general sense, how a survivor of child sexual abuse could so casually enter into multiple, unhealthy sexual relationships. You may also come away with a better understanding of just how devastating being victimized by a loved one is and how it differs from sexual assault from a total stranger. Returning to clergy sexual assault, this particular assault may feel more like that of a beloved family member, but only because of its exclusive nature. It remains an assault of a familiar association and a setting of intimate social contact.

Intimacy Learned

As a child of incest, I learned that one way to get someone involved or "groomed" for sex was to praise him with compliments and positive actions. Uncle Oscar, my childhood perpetrator, always told me I was his favorite nephew and that he loved me more than anyone. He often offered me back rubs as a child, even when I didn't want one, which gradually led up to full-body massages and mutual masturbation.

My uncle always presented himself as a caring and gentle person during molestations. In this perverse atmosphere, sexual encounters quickly grew to be my preferred alternative to the violent temper of an alcoholic father who seldom ever praised or held me. Uncle Oscar's indulgent message to me was, "you are loved, and you can only show love through sex, and above all, you don't have to be afraid." I was seldom afraid of Uncle Oscar's inappropriate touching or the genital manipulations he would perform on me to achieve a sexual climax, but I always felt confused and depressed after each episode.

Child Acting Out

Children often "act out" by harming themselves or others if they've been abused or are currently going through the abuse. Sometimes this acting out can be combined in their play. Several examples come to mind from my own experience. Parents of young children should beware of any sudden, unexplained changes in their child's behavior, attitude, or character. Be observant and go with your "gut feeling." and validate your intuitive sense as there could be recognizable signs of something more serious going on right in front of you.

I'll describe one childhood experience I recall that involved a neighbor friend, a boy with whom I was able to express my feelings of attraction. Manny and I were elementary school classmates, and I considered him my best friend. We walked to and from school and played together every day. Manny lived in a house directly behind ours, together with his single mother and three older sisters. I never knew where his father was.

One cold, cloudy fall day after school, Manny and I were jumping off my front porch to see who could land furthest away in the yard. The porch was about four feet high, and there was a nice, soft lawn for us to land on directly below. I remember feeling really happy that Manny was my best friend, neighbor, classmate, and playmate. I wanted to let him know how I felt.

Manny jumped off the porch first, but his feet slipped out from under him, and he landed flat on his back. He started to laugh, and so did I. He was laughing so hard he couldn't catch his breath. At one point, he lay back on the lawn and called for me to jump over him. I jumped off the porch and landed on both my feet right next to Manny. I stepped over Manny with one leg and stood directly over him.

As we continued to laugh at our behavior, I sat down on Manny's stomach. I reached out and took hold of both his hands, stretched them over his head, and instantly leaned in and kissed him on the lips. He struggled briefly, then quickly managed to force me over on my back, also pinning me by sitting on top of me. Manny held me in the same pose then proceeded also to lean in and kiss me back. I remember him pulling back, still holding my arms down, and looking me in the face and smiling.

It was a familiar, reassuring, accepting "everything's all right" smile of approval I had seen before from Uncle Oscar. I remember feeling happy, special and didn't want that moment to end. We lay on the grass, holding one another, for what seemed an eternity until Manny's mothers' voice called him in for dinner. I remember feeling how nice this was and how excited and happy I felt inside. I hated that Manny's mother had called him away, and I spent the rest of the night dreaming about that playful but powerful moment of intimacy between best friends. It also reinforced the belief that those feelings of physical arousal for Manny was OK and acceptable, just like how Uncle Oscar's kissing sometimes made me feel.

Manny and I never spoke about that moment or played that way again. I never knew if Manny was feeling something for me as I felt for him or if he was just copying what I had done.

Elementary school pic "Statistics estimate that one in six boys are molested before the age of 18".

In stark contrast to my memorable experience with Manny, I recall a horrifying experience with a fellow classmate's parent when she found out I had kissed her daughter during recess on the playground. I was terrified and traumatized by the harsh and severe reaction from my classmate's mother. I had been taught by my uncle's example that it was appropriate and acceptable to kiss someone you really liked or thought was "special."

It was morning recess, and everyone was playing in the school playground. The playground was a very large area of asphalt—no grass and a few benches huddled around a large shade tree. There were lots of faded yellow and white lines painted on the asphalt: hopscotch patterns, basketball boundaries, and large circles. The children used these circular patterns as a guide on May 1st morning for the annual May Pole dance.

A new girl was introduced to our homeroom class. Her name was Sylvia. I thought Sylvia was the prettiest and most beautiful girl I had ever seen. She was tall and slender, stood very proper and ladylike, wore dresses with lace and ribbons, and had jet-black hair that was always perfectly combed in a ponytail. Sylvia's dark brown eyes were large and round with the longest eyelashes I had ever seen. I was completely captivated by her.

Sylvia made me feel excited inside and happy, especially when she smiled at me. My stomach did somersaults when she said hi. I once gave her my 5 cents milk allowance because she forgot hers. I was happy she accepted it. I would have done anything for her! One afternoon, Sylvia was standing with her girlfriend near the swings, and I wanted to let her know that she was very special to me. I wanted her to know that she made me feel really good inside and I liked being around her. I walked over to where she was standing, and before she knew I was near, I kissed her on her cheek and shyly confessed to her that I liked her a lot. Sylvia was horrified! She immediately ran away from me and yelled that she was going to tell on me. I feared getting in trouble but didn't understand why. After all, I knew from experience that you kiss people who are "special" to you. I forgot about Sylvia's reaction and threat when another classmate challenged me to a foot race around the playground.

The next morning, as I was walking into the playground area, I noticed Sylvia and an older woman walking rapidly towards me. I tried to look away but noticed, out of the corner of my eye, that Sylvia was pointing directly at me and whispering something into the woman's ear. As I was about to pass Sylvia and the woman, I suddenly felt someone grab me by my coat sleeve and stop me dead in my tracks. That, someone, was Sylvia's mother and she began to scream and threaten me. She yelled, "Don't you ever touch my Sylvia again!"

The playground instantly fell silent as everyone watched and listened to the humiliating reprimand. I felt so ashamed. I didn't understand what I had done to make her so angry and upset. I felt my father's rage coming from this woman, and it terrified me. Sylvia's mother started to shake me violently, and as my classmates watched in horror, I started to cry. Sylvia's mother stopped and let go of my coat sleeve. I ran into the classroom and spoke to no one that entire day, not even my teacher.

After school, when I got home, I remember Mom asking me if I was all right. I lied and said I was fine. Fortunately, no school administrators or faculty witnessed the confrontation, and my Mom never learned about it either. All I could think about was what it was I did to Sylvia that was so terrible and upsetting. I really liked her and thought she was special. I could not ever look at Sylvia again or be anywhere near her for fear of another confrontation with her mother. This experience shattered my childhood sense of confidence about expressing feelings of attraction towards someone I liked.

CHAPTER 8

ADOLESCENCE

Enduring continued sexual abuse into adolescence posed an even heavier burden on me because there were certain physical elements that were, in fact, pleasurable. Let me explain. During the entire time I was being molested; I felt that it was wrong and that it was completely my fault. But because I was a healthy developing teenager, there were times when I experienced sexual arousal and pleasure. This is one of the most confusing and overwhelming experiences any male victim, gay or straight, encounters. This confusion is compounded when what my mind is directing, my emotions are dictating.

My mind senses that the sex I am experiencing with another man is wrong, but my body feels pleasure and exciting orgasms. This internal conflict leads to a very negative and confused self-image. I grew more and more anxious and apprehensive regarding what was normal and sexually appropriate.

Faced with a violent alcoholic father, a pedophile uncle, and the responsibility of protecting four younger brothers and sisters all living under one roof, I went through a great deal of emotional turmoil in my home life. At school, I was considered a model student, the perfect example of a high achiever. I never allowed myself to disclose any hint of my dysfunctional family, incestuous relationships, or violent home life to my teachers and classmates.

Many survivors of child abuse are taught to never question the authority of parents or elders, even when their actions are unjustified and abusive. As a child, when instructed to do anything by an adult, I obeyed without hesitation, no matter how painful or uncomfortable it was. I was afraid to do otherwise. This is what I was taught and why I believe the abuse continued on for all of my childhood years.

This was definitely the case within my family. Whenever we were in public or at family gatherings, we pretended as if everything was fine, which is typical of dysfunctional families. We laughed, we talked, we played, and we danced at relatives' homes. We were raised to be polite, respectful, and helpful children.

But this "Jekyll and Hyde" persona became unbearable for me, and at sixteen, with no end in sight to my absolute despair, I contemplated suicide. Fortunately, the attempt was unsuccessful. I then sought help from a local mental health clinic I found advertised in the local phone book, which offered free counseling services. Looking for other sources of support, I eventually became involved with a Christian prayer group on my high school campus. These two resources helped me begin to tolerate the emotional turmoil and traumas in life and lead me to cope with the nightmares at home temporarily.

CHAPTER 9

ASSAULT MEMORY

What follows is just one detailed assault I remember from my childhood but managed to lock away for years within my mind. If you are a survivor of such trauma, you know this all too well and should not read this experience. If you are not a survivor of sexual abuse, then continue reading because this is what's behind the humiliating secret of when an adult sexually assaults a child. Recounting this sexual assault leaves me emotionally raw today, as when it first occurred back in the 1960s. It is painful to read, but I share this in order to help other survivors with similar histories know that an emotionally positive and productive life can become a long-term reality.

I was not yet old enough to attend kindergarten, maybe about 4 years old, and at home all the time. I had just finished my lunch, which consisted of a tuna sandwich, strawberry Kool-Aid, and barbeque potato chips, and ran outside to play carrying my favorite bag of marbles. I remember using my fingers to draw pretend streets for the marbles in the dirt and used small rocks as make-believe people. After a while, I heard my mom calling me to come inside and take a nap. She said it would only be for a short time and that when I woke up, I could return outside again to play.

Uncle Oscar was outside sweeping the porch off when Mom called him inside, too, and asked him to put me down for my nap. Uncle Oscar held out his hand for me to take, and Mom ordered me to go with him. I hesitated, but Uncle Oscar took hold of me and lifted and carried me into my bedroom. I protested, insisting that I wasn't sleepy, but Mom insisted that naps in the afternoon were good for everyone, even her. She walked into her bedroom and closed the door. Uncle Oscar also shut the door to my bedroom and lay down next to me in my twin-size bed.

I faced the wall and pressed myself up as close to the wall as I could, almost falling in between the wall and the bed. Uncle Oscar moved close to me and pulled me against himself. He held one arm around my tiny chest and the other around my waist. Uncle Oscar started to caress me and rub himself up against me; I could feel his erect penis pushing out through his pants.

The next thing I remember is lying on my back, and my pants pulled down around my ankles, my t-shirt rolled up under my chin, and feeling wetness in my crotch. I remember opening my eyes to see the top of Uncles Oscar's head positioned down between my legs. He was sucking vigorously and drooling all over me with his entire mouth over my penis, testicles, and anus. His face was flushed red. I could see the sweat running down his forehead and on his nose. His eyes rolled back in his head, and he was snorting like a wild animal.

At one point, he held my hands down against my sides while he continued to manipulate me orally. Obviously, I did not understand what he was doing and grew more and more terrified as he continued. All I could think of while watching and listening to him was that he was eating me alive, that he wasn't going to stop, and I was going to die. The entire horrible experience seemed to go on forever. I held my breath and closed my eyes tight. Above the slurping sounds of being devoured, I could hear the theme song to a favorite childhood cartoon, Felix the Cat, playing on the TV in the next room. Suddenly, my legs trembled violently, my heart raced in my chest. I stopped breathing momentarily and felt myself "urinating" in Uncle Oscar's mouth. I felt something shoot out from my penis like urine, but I knew it wasn't that. Uncle Oscar looked me in the eyes, held the fluid in his mouth, smiled approvingly, and then swallowed it all.

I was shocked and overcome with humiliation for not controlling myself. At the exact moment of my first orgasm, I fixed my gaze on the plaid bedspread and matching plaid curtains in my room and forever retained this vivid, life-altering memory. Whenever I see plaid patterns or hear the cartoon theme song to Felix the Cat, I am reminded of this moment.

Shortly following my orgasm, Uncle Oscar's whole body shuddered as he knelt between my legs. He briefly held his breath, then quickly exhaled and let out a deep animal growl. I really thought he was going to throw up right then and there, but he never did. He had masturbated to a climax while on his knees at the foot of my bed. He quickly wiped me down, put my clothes back in normal order, turned my body and face towards the wall, and said, "Now, go to sleep." He whispered a promise in my ear to take me to the toy store to buy a new, big bag of marbles when I woke up from our nap. I believed, as a child, that Uncle Oscar would never physically cause me pain or make me cry. Uncle Oscar always told me how much he loved me, offered to help me, even gave me gifts, and took me to a nearby playground to play. I did everything to keep him loving me but felt I could never let him know how scared I really was. I didn't want him doing these confusing things to me in my bedroom, but I always ended up doing what he wanted.

Chapter 10

Flashback

Many years later, when I was an adult in my early twenties, the whole terrible incident would return to me and in a most unlikely place—a Sears department store! I vividly recall the day I walked through Sears's bedroom display and found myself standing alone, my eyes locked on a child's bedroom set ensemble. Unknowingly, I was about to mentally relive that horrific incident from my childhood—with the whole sexual assault materializing right in front of me. Everything in the display room—the bedspreads, pillows, drapes, even the small carpet—was decorated in beige, brown, and black plaids. The linen curtains and the plaid pattern of the curtains in the display were exactly like the ones that had hung in my old childhood bedroom. I was standing and gazing at the sacrificial room where my childhood had been ripped from my life! Suddenly, my stomach felt nauseous, and my limbs weakened. A familiar pungent odor wafted over my nostrils, and my mouth became dry.

In that instant, I recalled the physical sensations and the distinct body odor of my uncle during that specific assault while standing in front of a department store child's bedroom display. This experience was completely unexpected and overwhelming all these years later. I could smell Uncle Oscar's distinctive bad beer breath and the repulsive body odor of his unwashed private parts. I was actually sensing these deeply hidden, repulsive sensations from so many years before.

I had repressed the memory and the smells associated with the assault experience until this moment, as I walked through that department store. After all the years that had passed, I was emotionally impacted as if not a second had gone by. The trauma was still there; its memory had never left me. Shaken, I promptly left the building and soon after discussed this incident at length with my therapist.

Many of my memories of physical and sexual abuse remained lost, even buried; but years later, with the help of a qualified therapist, I was able to recall specific details of these emotionally impacting events. Many male survivors like myself feel emotionally stunned when repressed memories of abuse surface—even after years of therapy. What happened to us as children is never completely forgotten but are often locked away or vigorously ignored. From time to time, for one reason or another, our emotional scars get "scratched," and this is always disturbing. Mental and emotional memories evoke particular physical and emotional responses from past abusive experiences.

I refer to these instances as getting my "buttons" pushed. These buttons can be triggered by something as simple as hearing a particular word or a name, smelling a certain aroma or being in a certain physical environment or setting. To this day, when I hear the Felix the Cat theme song, my body instinctively reacts with a mix of unpleasant odors and uncomfortable body sensations.

Occasionally, in my adult life, a flashback relating to the abuse would suddenly occur when triggered by something unconsciously associated with the trauma, as happened to me years ago in a department store.

I have often been asked if I had lost any childhood memories due to the abuse. I remember only moments of my childhood; aside from the sexual abuse, I don't remember much. Most of my recollections tend to be of a childhood that was traumatic, of a family life surrounded by secrecy, sexual assaults, alcoholism, and physical violence. Even today, I experience huge gaps in my memory that are constant reminders of the emotional pain and distress that, as a child, I endured.

For the longest time, I thought that my abuse began when I was seven years of age. However, one day I was casually browsing through

a family photo album and discovered a photograph of the house where most of the sexual abuse took place. I looked at the date written in the photograph: "1961". I was five years old. I realized that I was only a child of five years old when the abuse began, two years younger than I had previously thought. Somehow, I had blocked the memory of a two-year span of my childhood, and I still have no memory of those two particular years.

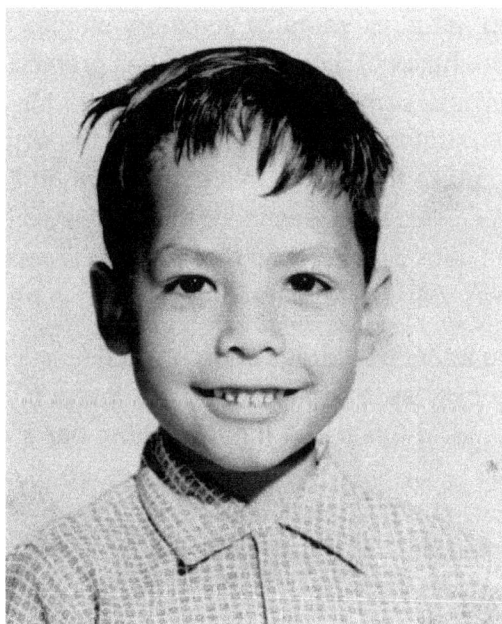

Me at age 5, when sexual assaults began.

CHAPTER 11

BACK TO A SECULAR LIFE

In June of 1980, after six years of seminary studies and four years shy of priestly ordination, I requested and was granted a formal leave of absence from the seminary and the Claretian Missionary Order. However, a few months before I was to leave the seminary, I asked for a temporary place to live in a Claretian parish in East Los Angeles—Our Lady of Soledad. It was there that I assisted with the church youth group and choir practice and met a young woman by the name of Ester. She was very polite, attractive, and fun to be around.

Together we attended various church youth functions and events. We grew close over several months, and I found myself waiting to see her alone after a function. I thought about her a great deal and felt that she was really special. Once I worked up the nerve to invite her out to dinner, she accepted. She reciprocated with an invitation to spend an afternoon at the beach. We became emotionally attached to each other, a special friendship developed, and eventually, we fell in love. I had been working at the parish while in the seminary and as a seminarian. I maintained a professional platonic relationship with Ester but, after I left the seminary, Ester and I started seriously dating.

We went everywhere and did many things together. I really enjoyed being with Ester: she was so loving. I couldn't help but fall emotionally in love with her. What I couldn't feel was sexual attraction toward her. We'd often lie together and kiss passionately, but it never went further than this. I enjoyed the tenderness and intimate touching and sharing we did while in each other's arms, and I responded physically with an erection to her sensuous kisses. She always said she was saving herself sexually for marriage, and, of course, I was relieved to hear that.

I thought she was THE woman for me; I fantasized about actually marrying her. Fortunately, a very wise therapist at the time opened my eyes to the reality of my own orientation and suggested I consider terminating the romantic aspect of my relationship with Ester and just allow her to be a friend.

I struggled with this for weeks before finally telling her that I couldn't continue an exclusive intimate relationship with here because I was gay. It was a tremendous shock and heartbreak for her, and she quickly disappeared from my life. I had never experienced sexual intercourse with a woman and now knew that it was never going to happen. Looking back, I'm glad I ended the romantic relationship. I was happy to hear, years later, that Ester found love again, married, and has a family of her own.

Over the years, many closeted gay and bisexual men who marry women consistently threaten the emotional, psychological, physical the health of their partners by secretly engaging in sexual relationships with other men.

For many male survivors of child sexual abuse, gay or straight, we have the additional challenge of controlling compulsive sexual behaviors which expose us, and our partners, to all forms of sexually transmitted diseases, many with life-changing and irreversible consequences.

It is my personal hope that every closeted gay and bisexual man living in a marriage with a woman, find courage by this honest conversation, to seek a better understanding of his sexuality in order to live a safe and healthier life.

Single & Gay

My dream of becoming a Catholic priest was completely destroyed by my sexual encounters with Father Raab. For six years of seminary life, I had been shielded from the secular, non-religious life-style. I realize now that perhaps it was just a matter of time before I accepted that being gay and trying to live a celibate religious life would, for me, be close to, if not impossible. I craved the physical and emotional intensity, intimacy, and sexual touch of another, exactly what I thought I had experienced that July 4th evening with Father John.

Now, I was also about to find out that, as a single gay man living in Los Angeles, experiencing that level of emotional intimacy would be equally painful and, more times than not, extremely disappointing.

I continued seeing a therapist for several months after I left the Claretian seminary. I was able to keep my employment position with the Archdiocese of Los Angeles as a sign language interpreter and religious education instructor for hard-of-hearing children. As the months passed, I found it more and more challenging to remain work-ing among clergy or within the confines of the Catholic hierarchy, so I decided to seek employment away from the church.

My outlook had changed radically regarding faith, the Catholic Church's moral teachings and how they viewed gay people. I had lived among gay priests and brothers, some who were in control of their sexual desires, others challenged by them, and some com-pletely manipulated by them. I had also begun to notice an atmos-phere of "don't ask, don't tell" secretiveness with regards to friend-ships formed between clergy administrators and seminary students, particularly those of us who were gay. While living at the seminary, I had observed priests in leadership roles, including Father John, pay-ing particular attention to one individual seminarian over another.

Private one-on-one strolls around the seminary property, an ex-clusive invitation to meet at a nearby restaurant, or a late-night meet-ing in the private bedroom of the priest director, were the most obvi-ous examples of these selective relationships. No one ever ques-tioned this behavior and most assumed that spiritual counseling and direction had taken place. Looking back now, I clearly understand that some seminary spiritual directors were inappropriately focusing their own physical interest and sexual attraction on certain individual seminarians.

Over the span of my six years in the seminary, I became the target of several other predator priests while studying to become a priest, both inside the seminary and outside. Most of these priests were older then me and were not as clever as Father John, but who took advantage of their authority over me and acted physically inappropriate.

I recall one specific instance, after being singled out by one spiritual director, where I was invited after dinner to visit him in his private room. Up to this point, it was something we had done many times without incident. We usually spoke about church-related topics, personal development, and academics with a lot of humor thrown in.

The atmosphere was always comfortable and welcoming. But suddenly, one night, we began to wrestle with each other playfully, and he threw me upon his bed. I thought it was simply horseplay, but this priest would not let go and held me in a fierce hold. After several attempts to escape his hold, I gave up and just lay there. At one point, this priest, while lying on his back, pulled and lifted me on top of his body. He covered my eyes with one hand and firmly held my forehead with the other. I could peer out between his fingers and could see he had a complete erection! I did not expect this from him; after all, he had been one of my spiritual directors during college. He noticed that I had seen his erection and released me. There was some embarrassment on his face, but he said nothing, not even "excuse me" or "I'm sorry." This was unexpected, and I felt betrayed and victimized. I left and never again returned to him for spiritual direction or anything else.

I distinctly remember that this priest seemed to favor his attentions upon a different seminarian, each new semester. It was so obvious to all of us students, just whom Father was going to spend extra, exclusive time alone with. I recently reconnected with one straight, a former seminarian who told me about his uncomfortable encounter with this same priest that also involved a playful episode of wrestling during an out-of-town trip. It appears to me that, in many cases, once we learn of a predator's method of making physical contact with a victim, there often seems to be repeating patterns of specific behavior, i.e., playful wrestling or back massage. As it turns out when we are able to recall and identify seductive behaviors used by predators, we find out that certain aspects of normally innocent behavior become key to understand how these situations progress into actual sexual assaults.

I have discovered through mutual acquaintances that this now senior priest is still in ministry and, over the years, continues to pursue multiple secret relationships with men.

I took the path to learn, observe, and think critically for myself, and to question and challenge the Catholic Church's self-declaration of absolute authority. I no longer felt I belonged and resisted accepting the moral sermons of hypocritical religious leaders who themselves were gay, "in the closet," and sexually active.

Despite years of emotional turmoil caused by my experiences with sexual predator priests and some notably disappointing responses from corrupt Catholic officials, I have miraculously managed to retain a secure personal and contemplative spiritual prayer life outside the church.

Coming Out Letter

I was becoming more and more confident with my gay sexual orientation and eventually gained the personal courage to come out to those closest to me, including work associates and relatives. I was no longer willing to remain secretive about something so important to my personal healing journey. I spent several weeks drafting various letters, trying to express exactly what I wanted them to know. Below is the letter I shared:

Dear Loved One,

You may or may not appreciate what I am about to share with you, but it is my feeling that if you and I are to continue to grow in our relationship of trust and love, as is my wish—then I want you to know and understand me better. I feel that we have grown in the time that we have known each other and I believe you have a good idea of what kind of person I am. I have come to a point in our relationship where I want to be more of myself with you in expressing my thoughts, feelings, and interests.

Up to now, I have had to guard some of what I feel like sharing or expressing with you—some things that are very important to me as a human being, a person, a man. I am not one to play games or be deceitful; that's not my "style." I am emotionally, physically, and sexually attracted to men. I have reached a point in life where I feel very comfortable and accepting of this. It is part of me and a large part of who I am. I have discussed this issue with several therapists over the past few years, both as a teenager and young adult. I have wanted to change, and wished I could change—I have wanted to be "normal" and not different—but you know what I Have discovered? I am normal; I don't need to change anything because my feelings are real, my emotions are positive, and my love is genuine.

Most importantly, I am happy and very comfortable with myself as I am. My need for love, companionship, trust, security, and stability are as common to everyone (men and women) as is the need for air, food, and water. My needs are better understood, accepted, and met by a person of the same sex with similar needs and experiences. I realize this may be very difficult for you to read, let alone understand, but keep in mind who it is that is writing this—me, someone you've shared time with. Being gay does not change me, nor my feelings for you. I am the same person now as I was before you read this.

I've chosen to be closer to you in our relationship by sharing (or, as the more popular term goes, "coming out") with you some more of who I am. I am prepared to accept your decision to continue or not continue deepening our present relationship.

All I ask from you is for you to be honest with me about how you feel about this. I would appreciate knowing right off if you are uncomfortable with or unable to handle this information. I would prefer that you told me now instead of gradually avoiding me or disassociating yourself from me. I can take it; believe me, I have known people who prefer not to deal with this topic on any level, and for now, I have to accept this. An honest and mature understanding is what I want between us. I have said all that I wanted to say for now . . . I have said a lot! How do you feel?

As I expected, most recipients were surprised but sensitive to what I was feeling. Several people expressed support, appreciation, and love for my having told them such a personal thing about myself. Nothing changed between us, and I felt relieved. A few individuals were not comfortable discussing this topic further, and I felt it was just as well since they were never really as invested in our friendship as they had pretended to be.

I have been repeatedly asked if being sexually abused by another male contributed to my being gay, and I say no. For me, while I was growing up, I remember being much more interested in watching male television show characters than females. I use to feel my stomach get excited watching early 1960's TV personalities like Sheriff John; Chuck Jones, The Magic Man, and especially Batman and Robin. I can remember as a boy, staring at the TV set, admiring their faces, smiles, bodies, and muscles. I never felt so emotionally excited watching any of the female personalities on TV. I knew that I was different but did not understand why.

If anything, being sexually molested by a man should have turned me off completely because having sex with my uncle was so disturbing and disgusting, and not something I wanted at all. It wasn't until I was in adolescence and could dictate when, where, and with whom I wanted to be sexual with, did I discover moments of physical excitement and sexual pleasure, or at least what I thought was pleasure.

Uncle Oscar and me, age 15, on a family outing.

Chapter 12

Romanceless Dating

After I left the seminary and quit my job with the Los Angeles Catholic Archdiocese, I took a wonderful position at the Braille Institute of America. I became a low vision consultant and was trained to access levels of impairments in order to make visual aid device recommendations. It remains today one of the most rewarding jobs I have ever had. I enjoyed weekly overnight trips to different communities throughout southern California, and I received travel stipends and could set my own appointment schedule. I truly enjoyed it and always looked forward to showing up for work.

In September 1980, I moved into my first apartment on the east side of downtown LA, several miles away from the seminary house of studies. The unit was situated on the third floor of the complex and had a breathtaking skyline view. It was a terrifying and exciting new move: to be totally independent and to live alone for the first time in my entire adult life. It was with the help of some family, friends, work associates, and my therapist that I found the support to adjust to my new socially single lifestyle.

As I grew accustomed to being out on my own, I gradually distanced myself from church-related events, including attending Mass and communicating with former religious community members. I did experience moments of sadness, even heartache at not being in communication with some of my former seminary housemates and no longer part of the unique family spirit we shared. I chose to enroll in evening continuing education classes at the local community college and sought out social group activities, which I'd read about in singles newspapers.

For about eighteen months, I focused on my job and maintaining my own apartment. I did not know the first thing about how to meet other gay people and was getting comfortable with just being alone, to come and go as I pleased when I pleased I certainly knew where the gay hustlers were but was not interested in just having sex. Instead, I was hoping for someone to date and fall in love with.

In therapy, I gradually became more and more confident about being a gay man and felt ready to explore the local gay scene and, maybe, find a permanent, long-term loving relationship. I tried going to gay bars and discos but was disappointed by the large numbers of men who, under the influence of alcohol, always seemed available and only interested in groping my body. I went to numerous adult bookstores and discovered free gay and lesbian community newspapers to read and found many interesting events and services advertised. At the back of each publication were classified ads listing those looking for relationships; most were sexual in content while others seemed genuinely sincere. I decided to try running a classified ad to see what kind of guys I might meet. I had never responded to or placed a classified ad of any kind, but I decided I had nothing to lose and a lot to gain.

I was so excited that the very first week the ad came out, and I started to receive calls. After an initial interview over the phone, I chose to meet only those who sounded sincere for coffee in a nearby neighborhood restaurant like Denny's or Bob's Big Boy. I discovered that most of the men who responded lied about their age, weight, et cetera, and were nothing like they described, while others just wanted to have sex right away. The two most disastrous encounters I had were with a very attractive guy who suffered from erectile dysfunction and another who was hypoglycemic and periodically went into unexpected fits of rage. I quickly ended both and the last one because it reminded me of my father and his uncontrollable public rages. The amount of time, energy, and patience it took to screen potential mates was overwhelming and very discouraging.

Single and living on my own.

I dated a few "professional" alcoholics who, despite being very sexy men, never seemed to sober up, no matter how early in the day I called. These dates never stood a chance either because they reminded me of my growing up in a family of alcoholics and were a guaranteed turnoff for me. I grew emotionally tired and physically frustrated with the cycle of dating disingenuous and self-centered men who were mainly out to get laid once, then move on to the next guy. This was not what I wanted nor with whom I wanted to be romantically involved.

Jess & Sergio

Only two out of several dozen gay men I actually met were worth the entire gay classified ad experience. They actually taught me invaluable life lessons about being a healthy, smart, and confident gay man. I am forever grateful to them for their friendship, patience, respect, and honorable love.

First, there was Jess, an attractive Latino man who was friendly, funny, and honest about everything, including telling me that I was "not his type" at our very first meeting. I was offended but curious about what his type actually was. Neither of us was physically attracted to the other, but we could relate to each other as gay Latino men searching for a single, committed companion and partner. We became instant friends, and Jess introduced me to the gay dance club scene throughout LA and Hollywood. We both loved to dance and sometimes would dance nonstop for hours! Jess didn't smoke or drink, and neither did I, so when we found ourselves in clubs where there was smoking, we just left and sought out dance clubs within well-ventilated non-smoking areas. Jess and I became constant dance companions on the weekends and so close that we could often say out loud what the other was thinking. I would have been completely lost and overwhelmed by the entire gay scene had it not been for Jess at my side.

Jess and I talked about everything sexual and in very intimate detail. I learned a great deal and welcomed his opinions and suggestions about being gay and out to family and friends. I felt like I was back living with my seminary roommates. I could ask Jess about anything, even the most intimate thoughts and questions anyone could ask another man—without feeling embarrassed or intimidated. These intimate discussions were immensely helpful, especially regarding emotional intimacy between men and sexually transmitted diseases. I grew to love Jess purely for his genuine friendship, openness, and sincerity.

We spent many times just laughing at gay life and the many humorous aspects of being gay men. At one point in our relationship, I invited Jess to move into my one-bedroom apartment because he needed to flee from a physically abusive partner. I helped him move in and gave up the entire living room to set up his humungous king-size water bed. Having Jess as my roommate and best friend for those few months gave me some of the best times of my newly independent gay life. I am proud to say that after all these years, Jess remains my closest and dearest family friend.

After Jess, I met Sergio, a truly generous man who invited me to rent a room in his home so that we could both save money. I actually met Sergio while I was a seminarian working at Our Lady of Soledad Parish in East Los Angeles. Sergio was very socially active within the life of the parish and was the elementary school principal there. He was an all-around professional person whenever I encountered him on parish property and around the school. Sergio loved his students and was always protective of them and his faculty. He often told me how much he relished his position and job as a Catholic school administrator.

When I first met Sergio, I did not know he was gay. I had a slight suspicion he might be because, on several public community events, I noticed a tall, handsome blond man often accompanying him. My suspicions were confirmed one festive night at an outdoor parish carnival. There was a rock band playing outside in the church parking lot. A large dance floor had been constructed directly in front of the stage, and everyone was dancing. I saw Sergio dancing with several students, and he was dancing as good as any gay man in the discos Jess and I had seen—possibly better.

I knew then that Sergio was gay because I've never known a straight man to dance with so much rhythm and style. I "came out." to Sergio, the next day and told him he was a very good dancer and I really enjoyed watching him dance. I sensed he was a little uncomfortable because he remembered I had once been a seminarian assigned to the parish, but he politely thanked me for sharing this anyway. Over the course of several weeks, our friendship grew even more honest and telling.

What I learned most from Sergio was that I could be gay, happy, and professional in my job without flaunting my sexuality. He seemed to have it all: the love and acceptance of his biological family, a handsome partner, a successful public job, and supportive friends and associates, all of whom seemed to accept him for who completely was.

I was encouraged and inspired by how he carried himself in public, at work, and around the confines of a Catholic parish. As with Jess, Sergio and I were never sexually interested in each other but could talk frankly about anything and everything.

I understood from these two particular gay friends that not every lasting gay friendship involves having sex together. I was so relieved to experience true friendship and intimacy without the complication of sex getting in the way. Sergio even helped me purchase my very first car after I left the seminary; he did all the negotiating and ultimately sealed the deal. I could have never done that on my own.

This was, for me, the beginning of a new personal understanding of intimacy, friendship, and love that had seemed impossible to have. Sadly, in the early 1980s, Sergio became the first of many close friends and family to die from AIDS. I miss him dearly, but I know his precious spirit remains forever close to my heart. I also know that the spirits of our love relations — their energy — remain with us through-out our mortal lives and that they will all be present with us upon our own death.

CHAPTER 13

MY LIFE PARTNER

By 1983 I was resolved not to date for a while, just hang out with my close friends and stay happily single. I focused again on enjoying my apartment and finding a better-paying job. Not only did I find a better-paying job, but I also met Antonio, the man who ultimately became my life partner.

I accepted a job as the assistant director of the education department with the American Cancer Society (ACS) in Los Angeles. Except for myself and two other men in the entire office, women held every other position at ACS. Antonio was the assistant director of the patient services department, and our office entrances faced each other. I did not think Antonio was gay because he told me about having a girlfriend at the time, and I never sensed anything "gay" about him. He struck me as just another nice straight guy. I was not physically attracted to or sexually interested in him at all.

I was impressed by Antonio's professionalism and his caring demeanor while assisting cancer patients. I could hear how sensitively he spoke with each patient and their families. He was always a gentle, caring soul and spoke tremendous words of comfort to his clients, like no other person I had ever known. It was a great emotional responsibility to counsel cancer patients, but Antonio was the best person for that particularly sensitive job. In addition to offering cancer patients the necessary supplies and referrals, Antonio made it a point to offer himself after hours should any patient need emergency services. He often went above and beyond his basic job description when it came to supporting clients and providing personal attention.

I truly admired how gently he handled each client he encountered and made it a point to tell him this after they left his office.

Today, as Antonio likes to tell it, he says he knew I was gay right away because when I arrived on my second day at work, I brought in several live plants to decorate the otherwise stark office and proceeded to "pretty up" space. Between us, we still laugh about this whenever this particular memory is shared. I do admit that I have always liked my work environment neat, organized, and attractive. To me, plants are comforting and pleasant to look at and always add life to an otherwise dreary office cubical. And I do admit that it doesn't hurt to "pretty up" things from time to time.

When I started the ACS job, I was involved with a very large, gay outdoor adventure organization that offered weekend camping trips all over the state. Upon my return from one of these weekend trips, I would share my experience with Antonio, leaving out all "gay"-related references. Antonio loves the outdoors as well and would share with me all the places he had been, asking if I knew the locations, which I didn't.

One day, after I had finished telling him about my latest overnight camping trip, Antonio invited me to join him on a drive out to Malibu Creek State Park. It was the location used to film the TV show MASH and big movie productions like Planet of the Apes. I have always been interested in, and enjoyed learning about, behind-the-scenes movie magic and visiting actual film locations, so this was a particularly exciting invitation.

I thought it very nice of Antonio to invite me and couldn't wait to visit this new place. Our outing was set for Sunday, September 11th, 1983, and it was a very dry, hot day. Antonio picked me up at my home and drove us out to the park. It was really beautiful and peaceful. I think because of the scorching heat that day; not many visitors were out. At one point, we came upon an artificial lake, complete with water lilies and cattails. The water was cold and murky, and we spontaneously decided just to remove our clothes and jump in to cool down. It was so refreshing to be floating in the cool water on such a hot day. It felt fantastic and, with no one else around—comfortably private.

I was feeling pretty lucky to have Antonio as a new social friend, in addition to being my work associate. I thought him to be very sincere, open, and trustworthy. I felt comfortable enough to want to share with him about my being gay. I told Antonio that I wanted to tell him something personal about myself because I felt close and comfortable with our friendship. He welcomed what I had to say. When I told him I was gay, Antonio's simple but deceptive response was, "Oh, I know some gay people. I don't have a problem with it."

I felt completely validated and accepted, and then I casually changed the subject. I was feeling confident in being forthright with him and thought he could also be another great person to hang out with. We spent the rest of the day hiking, exploring, and talking about many other things.

After dinner, we drove over to Malibu State Beach, and he surprised me with a bottle of wine he had packed in the trunk. There was a full moon that night, and we sat on the beach surrounded by huge rocks and boulders. We passed the bottle of wine back and forth between us. I wasn't much of a drinker, so even with the dinner we had consumed, I slowly began to feel the effects of the alcohol creeping up.

I was lying back on the sand and staring up at the moon when all of a sudden, Antonio leaned over and planted a kiss on my lips. It was completely unexpected, out of nowhere, and a total shock. He had never indicated any inclination or interest ever, especially throughout that entire day. He pulled back briefly to study my reaction, then smiled and gently caressed my cheek. I thought to myself, what a fantastic surprise! Neither of us said a word, but we both knew right then and there that this was something truly special and wonderful.

Hours went by under that bright full moon, with the soothing, gentle sounds of waves breaking only a few yards away from our feet. We made intense, passionate love that hot September night, and yes, it really was just like what you see in movies! It was incredibly romantic and by far the most romantic thing that has ever happened to me. This experience is one of the highlights of my life and will remain my most cherished.

It was all the passion and excitement I had longed and ached for but had accepted I would never experience again. I had stopped looking and searching for love, and then, without any indication, it jumped right out at me! A wonderful, honest, loving man to love me, and I him. At last, a real-life, romantic, life-changing experience during which I knew without a doubt that I was unconditionally loved.

Indecent Exposure

Antonio and I had been together for approximately one year. We had moved in together and started focusing on developing a comfortable home and long-term committed relationship.

I found myself occasionally frustrated with our sex life because neither one of us seemed to know what the other really wanted or expected, especially me. A lot of psychological as well as some physical baggage from my childhood sexual abuse surfaced and caused me to feel awkward and uncomfortable. At a certain point in the relationship, my personal reaction to sex with Antonio was similar to how I behaved during my molestations: I'd perform in total silence and end it with a quick orgasm. Antonio said nothing during these times. He would simply view my odd behavior as something I needed to work on, and then he would return to his normal routine. I began to feel like I was not special or appreciated during or after sex, and somehow I didn't understand the connection it had with my childhood abuse experience. In time, I began to realize that my uncomfortable reaction to the silence during sex reminded me of the sex I had experienced with Uncle Oscar. I realized that I was now re-expressing this in a silent, quick, and robotic manner. I sometimes didn't feel emotionally grounded or satisfied by our lovemaking because of the silence and mundane repetition of it all.

I found myself fantasizing about sex with loud outbursts of emotionally intense directives and sensuous coaxing and felt something was missing. This did not fit with Antonio's personality, and I did not have the emotional courage to talk directly with Antonio about my feelings or lack of excitement, so he knew nothing about this. During this particular period in our relationship, I found sexual gratification and release in looking at porno magazines and watching sex videos. I understand now that Antonio was experiencing similar frustrations but, like me, did not know how to approach the topic.

Once in a while, I would enjoy flirting with fellow coworkers and associates but never sexually acted out with any. I felt confident and assured that my compulsive sexual inclinations were in control and conquerable. Oh, was I wrong, and one day I gave into them with serious criminal consequences.

I had known about several gay male cruising locations in a popular, well-known park north of Downtown Los Angeles. I had driven by several spots I had heard about through the gay grapevine and newspapers, where gay men could make contact with others for anonymous sex. I had gone several times and had had, on occasion, brief sexual encounters with other gay men, usually in the form of oral sex and mutual masturbation.

That day, I had got off work early and decided to explore a new area of the park that was supposed to be very private, secluded, and easily accessible for quick sexual encounters. I parked my car and did not see any other cars in the area. I waited for several minutes then noticed some movement out of the corner of my eye. There was a young man slowly walking along the side of my parked car. He looked average and nodded hello at me as he walked into a thick grove of trees. I looked around and didn't see anyone else around, so I got out to follow the "cruiser."

I walked into the woods, following a narrow, well-worn dirt path that I thought was completely isolated and safe. The cruiser was nowhere to be found, but then I heard the snap of twigs breaking and saw him standing against a tree. He was looking right at me. I stopped and stared at him, waiting to see what he would do next. He smiled at me and reached both hands into his Levis pockets, and started casually walking away. I looked around and still saw no one else in the woods, just he and I. I walked slowly further up the pathway and stopped inside a small grove of trees. I was completely surrounded by a small circular grove of pines. At this point, the cruiser began walking closer to me and towards the grove, smiling with both hands still inside his pants pockets.

I felt that we were far enough away from the street now to have total privacy for whatever. I stood among the trees, and with our eyes locked on each other, I reached down and unzipped my fly. He stared a moment, smiled, then started walking directly towards me. I turned slightly and acted as though I were urinating. I did not expose myself. I wanted to wait and see if he would expose himself first.

As I looked up, I saw a second male figure cautiously approaching me from the opposite side, and I immediately zipped up my pants. In an instant, both men had surrounded me. One flashed the police badge while the other placed my hands together behind my back in handcuffs and informed me that I was under arrest for indecent exposure.

At first, I was stunned and then felt totally terrified! I was at a loss for words and said nothing. The officer proceeded to read my rights, and when he asked me if I understood, I simply nodded yes. I never heard a word either of them said after the handcuffs were slapped on my wrists.

All I could think of was having a police record for indecent exposure and what Antonio, my family, and my associates would think of me. It was the most humiliating experience of my life, and I started to berate myself in silence. That's what you get! I kept saying to myself . . . You're supposed to know better!

I was photographed, fingerprinted, then placed in a holding room. A million pieces of information and thoughts went through my mind, one right after the other. I could not finish a single thought because the emotional stress and fear kept interrupting my thinking. What was I going to do now? What was going to happen to me? Would I be labeled a criminal forever? Would Antonio still love me? Would he still want me? After a period of time inside the holding room, an officer came and told me I was allowed to make one phone call. I did not hesitate one second and nervously called Antonio.

I was released with a summons to court within a few weeks. I couldn't face Antonio when he came to pick me up because I was so humiliated and ashamed. Silence surrounded us in the car all the way home. I wanted to die. Later that evening, Antonio broke the ice and asked if I was ready to talk about it. He knew the silence wasn't helping, and I told him everything that happened. I apologized to him and asked him if he thought he could ever forgive me. He replied, "I forgive you, and I'll always love you." He said that we would do whatever we had to fight this. We hired an attorney who specialized in entrapment cases, and we successfully cleared the charge from remaining a permanent criminal record.

In Los Angeles County that year, there had been a series of successful lawsuits won against the police department for unlawful entrapment stings involving gay and bisexual men at known "cruising" locations throughout that particular park.

Since then, I have never again placed myself in such a vulnerable and dangerous position as I had on that day. The life-altering lesson learned? Not to let my sexual motivations dictate or encourage inappropriate and risky behavior in public. I have been challenged and propositioned to act otherwise in years since but was "knocked to my senses" at that time and have so far managed to avoid placing myself in a similar situation again.

Chapter 14

Survivor Identity

Survivors of abuse use the term "survivor" to signify that living beyond childhood abuse trauma is possible. Through all the hurt and shame we experienced as male children and adults, we continue to survive and heal childhood traumas. As adults, we have the responsibility to aid and support fellow survivors. Many of us take on the role of caretakers of other survivors and encourage them to reach comfortable levels of self-acceptance, confidence, and positive mental health.

Personally, the term "survivor" gives me a sense of accomplishment and a feeling of hope. I am aware that surviving childhood sexual abuse and assaults by priests in college will remain an ongoing, lifelong process of challenges throughout my life. I know the limited risks of disclosing my personal abuse history to strangers, but the rewards and inner peace I've achieved thus far are immeasurable. Yes, I am a survivor, and I invite others to join me on this journey of healing. I'm a man who has found ways to live beyond the subtle humiliation of the survivor label and be a full participant in life and community.

For years, it had been the general perception of our culture that once a boy had been molested, it was more than likely he would grow up to molest as well. In reality, not all males who were abused as children become abusers. On the contrary, many tend to become protectors of children. They become teachers and social workers, doctors and nurses; they choose "protective" careers. These men make the solemn vow as children: "I am going to make damn sure that what happened to me will never happen to another child." This is exactly what sparked me in my advocacy efforts to educate communities regarding male victims of child sexual abuse.

The belief that sexually abused males become abusers is based on very old, outdated statistical studies conducted in prisons and correctional environments that held convicted sexual offenders. These isolated research projects have spawned an erroneous impression that all male survivors of sexual abuse are degenerate walking "time bombs" set to go off at the first opportunity to assault a child.

For many, this prevalent attitude has hampered efforts to unite male sexual abuse survivors. As a group, we the "non-offending." male survivors must not be overlooked. We are a population that is much larger than most realize, and we have been held back by the fear that our communities automatically assume that we, too, will abuse children.

There is a definite need for more in-depth study and research into the area of "non-offending" male survivors of childhood sexual abuse. At present, there remains a lack of resource data and materials that specifically support non-offending adult survivors of abuse. It is no wonder that men are uncomfortable exploring positive avenues of healing from child sexual abuse when they find themselves frustrated and fearful over any attempt at disclosure.

I'm confident that my multi-leveled survivor story will positively impact and encourage other non-offending adult survivors of abuse to stand not with shame but with courage. The time is now, the call is for today, and each new, outspoken male survivor voice has a dramatic and positive impact on the safety of all children.

First Male Survivor Organization

I thought that I had reached my most powerful achievement when I was publicly recognized as a pioneer in the fight against male sexual abuse. In 1980, when I found myself speaking on television about being a survivor of incest and sexual abuse, I was told then that up until that moment, most survivors who were interviewed by the media were women. No man had ever appeared on television before as a survivor until I did. The reaction and attention were tremendous.

Letters and calls from all over the country reached me from other men with similar experiences, seeking support and assistance. I was overwhelmed and quickly found myself faced with the unexpected challenge of now being their spokesman.

After I disclosed to my family that Uncle Oscar had molested me and afterward did not receive the support or understanding I desperately needed, I felt completely isolated and abandoned. I needed to know that I wasn't seen as just another humiliating family problem or the "bad guy" for exposing Uncle Oscar as the predator he was. I had contacted several survivor organizations, but the majority was comprised primarily of female survivors; still, I read everything I could get my hands on. I changed the materials in my mind to read "male" survivor every time it said "female" survivor. I decided to start a support group for non-offending adult male survivors of child sexual abuse. This was to be as necessary for my own healing as it would become for male survivors across the country.

Without any counseling expertise to draw upon, I designed a classified ad for my hometown newspaper, announcing the formation of a support group for male survivors and listing my home phone number.

Looking back now, I took a tremendous risk in doing that, but I was desperate. I received several calls from men during the first few days of the ad and quickly summarized that I needed to be selective of which survivors would best suit my support group. After talking with several male survivors, it became clear to me that some had never spoken about their abuse, nor had they ever received professional counseling specifically for sexual abuse traumas.

I was not then, nor am I now, a trained, qualified therapist and could not see myself even attempting to counsel survivors. I added two key requirements for acceptance into my new support group that helped avoid catastrophes for the group. The first requirement was, you must have had, or are currently in, therapy specifically addressing your abuse history and present-day issues. Secondly, you cannot have sexually offended a child as an adult survivor. These two criteria immediately saved me a tremendous amount of grief and anxiety by maintaining the appropriate level of trust and support for group members. As with most start-ups, I provided all the materials, time, and energy out of my own living room and free of charge.

The local newspaper did a feature article on me and the new men's support group I was forming. Within several hours after that article appeared in the local paper, phone calls and letters began flooding in, the majority of which were from wives and female partners of their male husbands and boyfriends who were abuse survivors. It was clear that there needed to be specific resources for male survivors, regardless of their level of recovery or therapy, which meant that I needed further to gather whatever resources I could. I started to compile a list of local therapists, resource organizations, and mental health conferences from across the country that worked with male survivors of incest and sexual abuse. It was a daunting task but eventually became an invaluable tool for male survivors seeking help.

I soon found out that it wasn't enough to have a list of potential resources to give out; I also needed to spread the word to other communities that these resources were available. I started to receive inquiries from various media agents asking for interviews. I found myself suddenly faced with telling my personal story in newspaper articles and on live television, something I had only done once before.

I had to quickly learn about the media interview process, that everything recorded is edited down to a brief minute or single sound bite. I was frustrated for not being given enough time to say what I wanted or needed to say. Initially, when asked a question by a host, I responded with detailed explanations, attempting to explain the "whole" story. But, as I discovered, I was abruptly interrupted and "cut off," then "thanked" by the host. This left me feeling as if I were not allowed to express all the information I had to offer. I was alone and on my own, learning by trial and error, completely at the mercy of program producers and talk show hosts. As with anything that involves repeated practice, I learned to use brief, concise sentences to answer interview questions and actually became quite versed in the process.

Suddenly, I found complete strangers from all over the country who had heard or read something about my work with male survivors, wanting to make donations. I was not a "formal" nonprofit organization by any means, but I knew I had to consider becoming one in order to accept these desperately needed donations. Again, I had no knowledge of how to start a nonprofit organization or what that even involved.

All I understood at the time was that if I were a nonprofit organization, I could accept donations for the work I was now undertaking and not have to pay out of my own pocket, which I had been doing. I contacted the local State Tax & Revenue Department and asked for information on starting up and running a nonprofit organization. With manuals, applications, and suggested documents in hand, I read through the numerous forms and submitted said items for nonprofit status consideration.

By now, I was somewhat known from the TV and radio interviews I had given, and professionals in the counseling fields were calling.

They wanted to know how they could get listed as a therapy resource or where they might send a male survivor nearest them for counseling. It was with the support and willingness of several of these professionals that I was able to ask some to serve on the initial "Board of Directors" for my new nonprofit organization.

Thankfully, several had plenty of experience serving on various boards and were invaluable in the establishment of our nonprofit male survivor organization. I named the organization P.L.E.A., which stood for "Prevention, Leadership, Education, and Assistance."

I learned about a conference for Adults Molested as Children in San Jose, California, and signed up to attend. I did not know what to expect; I had never been to such a conference. It was the first national conference I had ever attended for survivors, both male and female. It was an eye-opening experience, and I finally felt validated by others with similar childhood histories.

It was here that I met Dan Sexton. Dan was a featured presenter at the conference and introduced himself as a male survivor and associate with ChildHelp USA. He presented a workshop that day exclusively for male survivors. And he just happened to be a very handsome young man and captivating public speaker. My first impression of Dan was that he did not "look" like someone who had survived sexual abuse because he was so confident, articulate, and able to talk openly about the details of his experience without becoming an emotional "basket case."

I was very impressed by his ability to recount painfully specific memories of his childhood sexual abuse experience very matter-of-factly, without breaking down and crying. He will never know just how much of a positive impact he made on me that first day. It was right after attending his tremendously freeing and uplifting presentation that I decided I wanted to do the same and possibly more.

I introduced myself to Dan and told him about P.L.E.A. and my work with non-offending male survivors. He praised and encouraged me and offered whatever help he could. He was highly influential in my motivation to learn to speak frankly and candidly in public about my own abuse experiences.

P.L.E.A. (Prevention, Leadership, Education, and Assistance) officially became a legitimate organization in March 1986 and operated as the first national nonprofit organization to represent non-offending adult male survivors of child sexual abuse, until June 1989. I personally continued to sustain the day-to-day operations of the financial organization from my living room, while the majority of donations went to the production, publishing, and mailing of a monthly survivor resource newsletter.

Through my work with P.L.E.A., I met many notable professionals of that time in the "survivor" fields, including Christina Crawford, Laura Davis, and Mike Lew, and I became an admirer of each one, for their personal dedication and contributions. I was fortunate to have had several opportunities to accompany them on various media interviews and workshop and conference presentations. I gained much insight and wisdom from observing each of them at a variety of public forums. Although I was not a Ph.D. graduate, a licensed psychologist, or even a successfully published author, they offered me, without prejudice, their unlimited support and encouragement. I am proud and grateful to have been recognized by them as a significant contributor to the founding of the first nonprofit organization for non-offending adult male survivors of sexual abuse.

From 1985 to 1997, I am proud to say that I acquired an enormous amount of personal courage, self-respect, and hope from working among male survivors and professionals in the recovery field. After several years of answering the same familiar questions about what happened to me, I decided to compile the most often asked interview questions and answers I knew and published them in a book.

In May of 1990, my partner Antonio and I self-published Recovery For Male Victims of Child Sexual Abuse. We had no idea of how to publish a book but felt confident that it would be unlike any "academic." survivor book then in print. On our home computer, I took to compiling all the public interviews I had given over the years.

We then hired an editor and typesetter and produced a modest 40–page booklet, complete with resources and presentation outlines. We presented the finished manuscript to a printing company, received a quote for its production, and printed 1,000 initial copies under a newly formed publishing company, Red Rabbit Press. We had no idea how many we might be able to distribute or even how to get the word out. I literally took copies of my book to bookstore buyers, bought booth space at survivor conferences, and designed ads for print in various recovery organization publications.

The initial 1,000 copies sold out from these ads and at survivor conferences. In January of 1994, the booklet was reprinted into a new, expanded book, and an additional 5,000 copies were reprinted. Book reviews were favorable and encouraging as well as the hundreds of letters of support and thanks I'd received from survivors and their loved ones who had been moved and inspired by the book.

Today, the original Recovery for Male Victims of Child Sexual Abuse book is permanently out of print, but portions of it have been incorporated into UnHoly Communion. This book remains my sincere attempt to provide the reader with enough knowledge, confidence, inspiration, and self-motivation to step up and speak out against sexual predators and those who protect them.

Adult Relationships

Being sexually abused as a child affected my attempts to develop healthy adult relationships, particularly during my college years. As a child, I erroneously learned that in order to be loved, I had to perform sexual acts. This reasoning, ingrained in me for over fifteen years, stayed with me. As a result of this extensive early training, I found myself later as an adult acting in risky, inappropriate, and physically unhealthy ways.

My college and seminary years, as for many students, were a time to explore and mature sexually. As you have already read, on several occasions, I became sexually active with fellow classmates and several Catholic priests. I mistakenly reasoned many times that in order to maintain any sense of friendship or to retain their interest in me, I had to initiate and perform something sexual between us. I subconsciously believed that my sexual prowess would remain the primary reason anyone would be in the least interested in me. And so, for quite some time, establishing long-term friendships without a sexual element was virtually impossible in my mind.

The few relationships that did develop during that "coming out" year did not last due to this childhood misconception of what it meant to be physical with, liked, and accepted by another person. I seriously thought that if someone did not want to have sex with me, it was because I was worthless. For me, affection and love had to include inappropriate sexual intimacy—a way of thinking that I carried with me well into adulthood.

Unfortunately, for many adult male survivors, promiscuous, compulsive behavior with both men and women is another common means of not dealing with our unresolved psychological and emotional abuse issues. Relationships suffer, marriages dissolve, and families break up over compulsive sexual behavior that is usually hidden or ignored.

It has taken years of self-examination and discovery for me to realize that loving someone does not require a sexual act and that the basic act of sex should not be confused with love. At present, I attribute my continuing recovery to the fact that I can talk openly about my insecurities and concerns with my partner, share mutual experiences with fellow survivors, and know that, ultimately, sexual behavior healing is possible with additional counseling, the support of loved ones, and the survivor's willingness to always pick himself up whenever he fails to control those reoccurring periods of compulsive sexual behavior.

Sexual Identity Issues

There is no clinical research to support the idea that a boy molested by a man will himself become a homosexual in his sexual orientation. Male survivors may secretly "act out" physically and sexually with other men but not necessarily identify themselves as exclusively attracted or orientated to men. Heterosexual men who were molested by men as children worry if they are gay. Some gay men wonder if they are gay because a man molested them. Gay men have also expressed anxiety, wondering if they were, in fact, molested because they were born gay.

As I have stated earlier in the book, I remember at a very early age being fascinated with watching commercials with spokespeople and TV news reporters who were men. I also remember in kindergarten, being more interested in certain male classmates and wanting to sit close to them. I didn't understand back then why I was so excited to be friends with just male classmates and not with any female classmates.

Since preschool, I have always been physically and emotionally interested in having only male companions. Being gay was not something I had learned during my abuse experiences, but it caused tremendous confusion in my psychological and emotional development. If anything, there were certain sexual acts performed on me when I was a child that most gay men find enjoyable, but I did not. Although, as a child, I was repeatedly groomed and instructed to perform oral sex on older males, it remains something I do not particularly enjoy doing. As a sexual abuse survivor, I have had to find psychologically safe and physically comfortable ways of enjoying sexual intimacy with my partner.

I want to stress here again that being sexually molested by a male perpetrator DOES NOT automatically mean that a boy will grow up to be gay. A male survivor is inevitably faced with having to sort through a multitude of sexual experiences and behavioral conditioning before arriving at a comfortable acceptance of his sexual preferences and identity. I find that it is simply unproductive when values such as normal or abnormal, natural or unnatural, moral or immoral, are forced upon male survivors trying to make sense of their sexual preferences and orientation.

A male survivor must be cautious about conforming to standards established by social and religious conservative groups regarding the definition of what "normal" means. The objective opinions of a qualified therapist can be instrumental in assisting an individual in the clarification and understanding of his sexual abuse history, preference, and identity.

One of the long-term consequences of being abused as a child is a serious lack of trust towards adults and "authority" figures. This happens particularly when the perpetrator is a trusted adult with authority over the victim, someone the child may love and lookup to. An internal conflict develops as to how feeling love and showing love become issues of distrust and uncertainty.

Trusting someone later as an adult becomes confusing to survivors of sexual abuse. Understanding the concept of love can be the most difficult to comprehend. Adult male survivors find it difficult to make or keep new friends. Problems with trust and intimacy regularly occur, a result of repressed, negative associations that are unconsciously triggered by the possibility of an intimate encounter.

As an adult survivor, I was completely surprised when another type of "trigger" experience occurred between my partner and me. It happened when he first whispered "I love you" to me during one physically intense moment. I felt numb, lost my erection, and pulled away. My partner was never more sincere or "in love" than at that moment and was genuinely expressing his intense love for me. In my mind, I was once again reminded about all those times Uncle Oscar whispered in my ear, "I love you," while molesting me. I felt betrayed and emotionally upset each time Uncle Oscar said "I love you" to me during sex. When my partner said this to me, I froze and became that "dirty little boy" who did "nasty" things with his uncle. I did not expect this to happen and was upset at what I was feeling.

Again, my therapist-assisted me and encouraged my partner and I to discuss this in-depth so that neither of us would have to experience that uncomfortably awkward reaction again during sexual intimacy.

Today I can embrace my partner and whisper, "I love you," because not a day goes by that I do not feel his profound love and respect for me. I am cherished, and because I always feel it, I can confidently express my love in return.

As you might imagine, unexpected, negative survivor reactions towards a partner can be confusing, frustrating, and even cause partners to separate. It is important that survivors of abuse learn to identify just what their emotional "buttons" are and how these hidden triggers can easily escalate into serious arguments. We need to try to understand which type of behaviors or physical settings make us most uncomfortable, emotionally disturbed, or physically upset. It helps if you can recall your reactions and trace, whenever possible, those responses linked to past abuse experiences. Not a task for the "faint of heart" by any means, and ideally with the help of a qualified male survivor counselor.

Once these "buttons" are identified, we can practice moving beyond the emotional barricades that result from triggered subconscious memories. In order to move beyond these barricades, we have to allow ourselves the right to recognize and "claim" these past feelings by reprocessing our thinking for the present. It's so easy to stay stuck emotionally and do nothing to stop the disabling pain; to just feel that you can tune yourself out, be completely alone, and avoid having to confront the assault memories and all the emotional and psychological torture you experienced. I speak from experience when I say there is no other way to heal: each one of us who has found inner peace and healing has had to confront every intimate and disturbing issue one or more times. Today, online, there exists an abundant listing of resources for qualified, professional counseling services, local support groups, and organizations exclusively for male survivors, and I encourage you to take full advantage of them. There are also several nationally known male survivor support organizations listed at the end of this book for your consideration. I have had to learn, over the years, appropriate ways of expressing my own uncomfortable feelings of fear, anger, distress, and anxiety. This remains an ongoing exercise for me and requires daily practice.

Most of us who have survived childhood sexual traumas are well aware of those places, situations, and things that can "trigger" our senses and upset us.

For those of us who have been fortunate enough to experience healthy, constructive therapy, we have learned to identify those things that connects us to our childhood pain and have been taught new ways to address them directly. The fact that I have spent, off and on, several intense years in therapy does not exclude me today from moments of emotional sorrow, anxiety, or insecurity.

Male survivors of abuse may create mental walls between themselves and their past; they become numb to their feelings. They resort to a number of numbing strategies, which often involve alcohol, drugs, compulsive sexual behaviors, and eating disorders. Others choose more socially acceptable forms of, such as becoming workaholics, super athletes, and ultramarathon runners. They try to both numb and compensate for the pain, which in turn offers them a false sense of protection from their molestation memories.

Like most people living with a shame-based secret past, survivors can perform exceptionally well on a daily basis, among our associates, friends, and family, with seldom a hint of our scarred history. Every day, we are capable of providing for our basic physical needs, personal grooming, and social interactions. At work, we are viewed as competent workers, socially responsible, and comfortable to be around.

However, there remains the hidden, deeply intimate side of each of us that continues to hold on to memories of our sometimes humiliating compulsive behaviors that often prevent us from further healing and remain potentially dangerous, even destructive, to our lives and families.

My adult life has continued to challenge me as a survivor to fight the dysfunctional urges of compulsive sex that only put me in dangerous, vulnerable situations, which in turn result in my being psychologically manipulated, emotionally tortured, and molested all over again. This then gives into defeatist self-pity, self-loathing, emotional meltdowns, and other unhealthy, temporary distractions, such as compulsive eating, shopping, gambling, online chatting, pornography, and substance abuse.

Most of the time, I am hopeful, inspired, and satisfied by the wonderful accomplishments and successes in my life. I continue to learn, often painfully, how to look beyond my own insecurities and fears. I am repeatedly challenged to stop what I am doing and reaffirm to those I love that I do appreciate having them in my life and thank them for the love and trust they so generously gifted me with. I experience greater confidence in myself with each compulsive, sometimes addictive hurdle I overcome.

As a result of keeping our abuse histories secret, survivors often struggle with a frustrating, negative self-image. Most of us have periods where we often consider ourselves stupid, unattractive, weak, disturbed, and sick. Some adults have carried the false and overly simplistic rationale from childhood that they would not have been abused in the first place if they were more intelligent or better looking.

The effect I personally carried into adulthood was not being able to trust men or women in positions of authority. Trust was totally violated time and time again during my childhood by adult heads of household. To express genuine love and to feel free to be loved, to be involved in an intimate relationship emotionally and physically always seemed impossible to obtain from the adults I grew up with. The therapy proved extremely helpful in bringing down the walls that I had built to protect myself.

It is important to understand that there is hope for male victims of sexual abuse, as well as for all adult survivors. But first, you must seek out the support of other male survivors to share your experiences and participate in therapy with a qualified professional to address specific abuse traumas you have survived. You need to know that you are not alone. Healing the painful parts of yourself is possible when you're able to open up to finding a survivor support group, sharing your story with other survivors, and getting yourself into therapy. This is where most of us start our recovery process of healing.

CHAPTER 15

NON-SEXUAL ABUSE

Sexual molestation wasn't the only form of abuse I experienced in childhood. There was verbal, emotional, and physical abuse. Verbal abuse took place each time my father screamed at, threatened, and insulted me. Whenever my father drank alcohol, he always had something abusive to say. He repeatedly threatened me with the following: "You disgust me, and if you ever get in my way, I'll kill you." The most terrifying words I ever heard him say, accompanied by a cold, dead look in his eyes that I will never forget for as long as I live. He stood inches from my face, and I believed him.

Emotional abuse was sometimes subtle but equally vicious. When Dad was sober; he gave me money and complimented me for being helpful around the house. But within an hour, after a few shots of whiskey, he would summon me and lecture me about my "laziness." and "smart-ass attitude." I often felt like a ping-pong ball being whacked back and forth across a table, never knowing what to believe, always uncertain of how he actually felt about me. I learned not to trust the nice things he sometimes said and to expect put-downs and threats instead. I was left to second-guess what he really wanted or expected from me and did my best to act accordingly. Needless to say, I still fall into second-guessing myself when it comes to stating my opinions, explaining decisions, and confronting uncomfortable interpersonal situations.

Holy Confirmation

The worst experience of emotional abuse took place when I made my Holy Confirmation in the Catholic Church. I was in my early teens and had been attending a confirmation preparation class for several weeks. I knew I had to ask someone close to me who was a practicing member of the Catholic Church to be my sponsor. The confirmation sponsor's role was not only to stand publicly by me at the altar but also to encourage me further towards deeper spiritual development and faithful participation in the church. I was happy and excited to finally finish my academic preparation for this event and know that all my family would be in attendance. I had to carefully select someone really special for this Holy Confirmation day.

To my horror, my parents proposed and insisted before a room filled with relatives that Uncle Oscar be my Holy Confirmation sponsor. They proudly announced to everyone that he has always been around for me, done things for me, and loved me. I felt sick. They obviously did not know just what he had actually done to me in the years leading up to that day.

I declined as politely as I could and resisted, claiming that I had someone else already in mind. Uncle Oscar was grinning and acting proud as he stood beside me with one arm wrapped around my shoulder. My parents did not accept any opposition to their choice and thought I was ungrateful and mean-spirited. I even managed to express my dissatisfaction directly to my uncle about his involvement. Still, he, too, persisted in his desire to be my Holy Confirmation sponsor. He knew I had no choice and continued to play along with my parents until I gave in. Ultimately, I was outnumbered and overwhelmed by the pressure from my parents and Uncle Oscar and caved into their emotionally devastating request. I despised Uncle Oscar for doing this to me and hated the very thought of him standing next to me at the altar in the church.

On the day of my Holy Confirmation, while Uncle Oscar stood painfully close to me on the altar, my eyes welled up with tears as I shook with rage and hatred. I felt trapped and was silently screaming from a torturous black hole deep within me. I wanted to disappear from the entire planet forever but couldn't. I felt stripped naked before the entire congregation of onlookers, parents, siblings, relatives, and friends. I just knew that they could see that Uncle Oscar and I were having sex. Everyone had to know by now and could see the guilt all over my face. I was sure of this! I was especially petrified by the thought that even the attending cardinal and priest standing around us on the altar could see that Uncle Oscar and I were sexually involved, but they too chose to simply go on with the ceremony anyway. This would remain one of the absolute worst public days of my young life. It truly was.

"I just knew that they could see that Uncle Oscar and I were having sex".

Now, our secret was not only being ignored by my parents and family, but also by my church! Their silence seemed to condone the sexual assaults by Uncle Oscar, even as he professed before God and the entire congregation to be my confirmation sponsor. The sickest thing about being so visibly public in church with my perpetrator was that the day before this momentous occasion, we had sex in my parents' garage.

Except for the act of physically standing next to my perpetrator on the altar with his hand placed on my right shoulder during the entire ceremony, I do not remember anything else about that day. I will never forget feeling like a complete church fraud and social freak before the congregation. This was the final contributing factor at the age of 16 that pushed me into a hopeless mindset towards suicide.

THE HOLY SACRAMENT
OF
CONFIRMATION

This is to Certify

That _Henry Estrada_

The Son ⎱ of _Tony Estrada_
~~The Daughter~~ ⎰

and _Alice Lozano_

baptized on _May 20_ 19 _56_ in the Church of _Our Lady of Solitude_ , _Los Angeles_
city

received The Holy Sacrament of Confirmation

on _December 9_ 19 _69_ in the Church of _St. John the Baptist_ , _Baldwin Park, Ca._
city

by The Most Reverend _Joseph Dougherty_

Sponsor was _Oscar Estrada_

Rev Raphael R Sweet Pastor
(asst.)

Date _September 8, 1971_

© Benziger Brothers, Inc., 1967   Form No. 3433   Made in U.S.A.

Confirmation Certificate

Of course, the most visibly recognizable form of abuse is physical, but one I managed to avoid while growing up. A child with scars, bruises, cuts, burns, even dislocated or broken bones are nowadays

116

often looked upon with suspicion. I was an abuse victim of less physically identifiable indicators but more frequent physical assaults, which involved slapping, shoving, violent grabbing, and shaking. Hair and ear pulling and pinching are also common forms that do not necessarily leave identifiable marks.

In my home, my father resorted to various methods of "discipline." He would violently shake my mom or me while standing with his face right up in our faces. Sometimes he would grab me by the arm and pull me hard towards himself. When I was twelve, I vividly recall defending my mother from my father during one of his physical assaults on her. My father and I were standing up near a large sliding glass patio window when I screamed at him to stop! He slapped my face up against the sliding glass door, glaring at me and saying, "I dare you to start crying." I saw stars the instant my face hit the window, and my knees weakened from the unexpected blow. I stood staring hatefully at him with clenched teeth as the painful sting overtook the side of my face that hit the window, followed soon after by the other side where he first hit me. Tears welled in my eyes, but they never fell. He walked away, and that violent episode was over.

CHAPTER 16

PERPETRATORS

I've often been asked if there is a difference between being abused by a family member or acquaintance versus a stranger. I think there is a difference. A pre-existing relationship of intimacy and trust exists with a family member, be it a mother, father, sister, brother, or, as in my case, an uncle. With a stranger, feelings of intimacy and trust do not necessarily exist. However, a child can develop a similar trusting friendship with an authority figure, e.g., a teacher, neighbor, or clergy person, which does not pre-exist as with a family member. When a family member connected by blood or marriage violates a child, the level of psychological trauma is intensified by the emotional depth and degree of their relationship.

However, this level of intense emotional intimacy usually does not exist on as powerful a lever as with a stranger. The abuse might be equal in its physical repercussions but not necessarily as emotionally or psychologically damaging as when perpetrated by a close family member. Understandably, the long-term emotional and psychological effects are enormous on any young victim who has been taught to love and trust an individual who later sexually abuses them.

If the perpetrator of sexual abuse is female, there is still today a "double standard" perception. As a boy matures and learns society's definition of what a "man" should be, the reality of his abuse experience becomes even more confusing. Males in our society are expected to explore and be ready for sex all the time, provided it is "normal." sex between a man and a woman.

The abuse by a female on a male child is romanticized and generally defined by society as an initiation into manhood. On the other hand, if he experiences pleasure or enjoys any part of it, he might not perceive the incident as sexually abusive. If the experience was not enjoyable, the boy might develop a confusing sexual self-image and very often think of himself as possibly being homosexual.

The consequences of being sexually abused as a child, either by a woman or a man, remain the same later in life. It may be manifested as sexual dysfunction, a lack of trust, or a negative self-image. If the perpetrator is the boy's mother or father, it is more likely that the child will block the memories. For the most part, because a parent's role is supposed to be protecting and nurturing, the child may rationalize the traumatic experience to the point that it is forgotten or convinces himself that it "never really happened."

Sexual abuse, whether experienced once or multiple times, leaves a tremendous amount of psychological "baggage" on all victims. A single act of abuse can traumatize a person physically and emotionally as much as often-repeated assaults can and do. By the same token, a child's testimony of having been abused should never be trivialized or discounted. Communities need to investigate any and every alleged act of sexual abuse vigorously and completely, no matter how uncomfortable, awkward, and sensitive these confrontations may be.

All survivors carry reminders of this experience throughout life, usually in the form of shame, guilt, and fear. The conscious act of keeping silent is an attempt by the victim to cope with the abuse. In my situation, as a child, my right to tell was taken away by an adult whom I trusted and loved. The subject of sexual abuse or alcoholism was never permitted or discussed in our household but was, in fact, avoided and ignored. When the assaults began to occur, I was forced into sexual compliance by my uncle, who acted and hid quietly behind my family's avoidance to confront suspicious, inappropriate behavior.

All I wanted was to be loved and to show love in return. I did, however, fear telling friends and classmates because I knew deep down in my heart that it was wrong and dirty, and they would know how "sick" I was for having sex with my uncle. Despite being told repeatedly by Uncle Oscar that what we did together was special, I still felt shame. I also feared telling my parish priest and religious instructors because I learned from church lesson plans that God would stop loving me for sinning, and I would never be allowed in church again or, for that matter, into heaven when I die. Surely, I thought, the gates of hell would have been unlocked just to receive me.

I feared telling my teachers because they would certainly want to discuss the matter with the police. I would then have been in serious trouble with my father for telling on his brother. I thought that in his rage, Dad would have beaten both me and Uncle Oscar to death.

This made it extremely difficult to love and trust people who said they loved and cared about me. None of them could protect, help, or save me. At a very early age, I felt completely alone, somehow responsible, and saw no alternatives for getting away from this tormented home life.

My response, and the typical response of others in my situation, remained the same: I kept the violation to myself. I kept quiet. I hoped that by not disclosing the abuse, it would simply go away. One can then understand the mixed emotions that confront an abuse victim. These emotions, however, do not disappear. Instead, they build and eventually become irrepressible.

Society today has yet to completely accept the concept of males as victims. However, it continues to get better. For most people, the term "victim" conjures up images of a "helpless female" being confronted by a male assailant. To have been victimized as a child, an adult male must confront various prevalent "mindsets." Our culture also influences males to think of sex in terms of whether it was easy to get rather than if it was a negative experience. Boys are often told, "Why complain? You just started earlier than most boys. Aren't you the lucky man?!"

We have to continue to combat social attitudes regarding male victimization and realize that children can become manipulated and coerced. Re-education is key for the healing process that we, as abused males, must confront every time we elect to speak openly about our humiliating experiences. When a boy is victimized, he is treated and often perceives himself as less than a man: effeminate, weak, or inferior.

Males today, even if they are young boys, are still expected to stand up to bullies and confront and control adverse situations, whatever they may be. Society then needs to develop a clearer, more constructive, and objective view of the abuse of males if prevention and recovery are to be successfully attained. The importance of male-specific open dialogue, intervention, support, and accessibility to qualified professionals in the field of sex abuse recovery will directly impact the healing of males in the future.

Confronting Perpetrators

Should survivors confront their perpetrators? I say that the decision is an extremely serious and complex one and must be left up to each individual. A substantial amount of mental and emotional preparation must take place before a survivor attempts to confront his perpetrator. The foremost reason is to prevent further victimization by the perpetrator and/or their defenders, which may continue thereafter in any number of ways.

Perpetrators, and probably also sociopaths, rely on the emotional and psychological mastery they hold over their victims. They may deny any connection with the survivor's attempts at disclosing the abuse to avoid confrontation. They may even gain the trust and favor of family and friends and turn these people against the survivor.

It is therefore essential that adequate psychological preparation, along with emotional support, exist prior to any confrontation attempt. The survivor's fears, concerns, and actions need to be discussed with a qualified therapist. It is imperative that he speak with other survivors who have actually confronted their perpetrators. I suggest role-playing the various scenarios that may transpire during a confrontation. Survivors have to decide for themselves just what they expect the confrontation will accomplish and what their own reactions will be if they do not receive the answers or responses they expect.

Unexpected Confrontation

I believe that the overwhelming number of letters of support and encouragement from fellow survivors over the years influenced the unexpected confrontation I had with Uncle Oscar while at my parents' home. The thought had never occurred to me to confront, or even speak to him after all these years, but I did.

The confrontation with Uncle Oscar was not planned and occurred spontaneously. He was now accustomed to leaving the house whenever I arrived for a visit. I never acknowledged his presence; yet, he would always greet me with a guilty and cautious "Hello." Uncle Oscar went out of his way to be the "nice guy" in front of everyone, while I was regarded as the cold, rude, and inconsiderate nephew. No one knew about my sexual assault history with him; they only observed our uncomfortable and brief salutations.

I resented being thought of as "the bad guy" while Uncle Oscar was seen as an angel of innocence, glowing in the eyes of relatives and friends. I was totally disgusted and outraged at the mere sight of him.

On this particular afternoon, I exploded in disgust at his "holier than thou" attitude. I cornered him outside in the garage of my parents' home when we were alone. I was shaking with rage. My stomach convulsed as I stared directly into his eyes. I pointed my finger in his face and threatened him: "If I ever hear about you touching anyone, I will." I never finished the sentence, but I know he understood the intent. I gave him that same hate-filled death stare that my father had given me.

After what seemed an eternity of me staring him in the face and his silence, I said, "Do you understand what I am saying?" In shock, he nodded yes. I squeezed my hand into a tight fist, held it close to his face, then turned and walked away. Naively, I assumed it was now possible to put the entire incest and sexual abuse history behind me and move on.

Those who decide to confront their perpetrator should prepare a final statement to close and terminate the confrontation. I thought of a million other ways I could have ended the confrontation, after the fact and what specifically I could have said but did not. Afterward, I thought of so many things that sounded much more complete and concrete, but I had been too overcome with rage to think these at the moment.

Ideally, the confrontation should be a clarification and statement of some of the following points made directly to the perpetrator:

1. "You sexually molested and abused me."

2. "I did not deserve to be molested by you."

3. "I am not responsible for your molesting me; YOU are!"

4. "You betrayed my trust and love for you."

It should be noted here that many survivors have achieved personal healing through their recovery journey without ever confronting their perpetrators. They have found their own method of coping and healthy, comfortable sources of refuge. Confronting the perpetrator is not necessarily for everyone, but for some, it has proven instrumental in their ability to move on and feel they are healing.

Finally, for those survivors not even close to confronting a perpetrator and who are still hiding their sexual abuse history, I must ask: "Do you realize now who you have actually protected by remaining silent? It is your abuser. And more importantly, after you kept quiet, do you know how many other innocent kids unknowingly become victims of your perpetrator?" Truly, a sad reality, but one that you can prevent from happening or continuing to happen if you identify who molested you. It's not too late. Please, you have to tell others what happened to you and name who it was.

Uncle's Gilbert's Revelation

I had become fairly proficient with public speaking and delivering workshop presentations. My life and nonprofit work had been the topic of many articles, talk shows, and radio interviews. One late morning, after I had completed a TV interview in Los Angeles, I received a phone call that I will never forget.

The male voice on the other end of the line sounded vaguely familiar, but I could not place it. After a long, silent pause, the voice identified himself as a long-lost uncle. Uncle Gilbert was my father's and Uncle Oscar's youngest brother. I carry only fond childhood memories of Uncle Gilbert and consider him my personal favorite. He was always fun to be with, very energetic and brought much joy to my life whenever he was around. However, the older I got, the less he would attend family gatherings or special events.

I recall the last time I saw Uncle Gilbert was after a particularly vicious and violent physical fight he and my father had on the front lawn of our home. Uncle Gilbert had attempted to physically defend my mother from my father's violent assault, and my father attacked him. It was a horrifying scene witnessed by guests and neighbors. It was a Saturday night, and we had a house full of visitors, gatherings our families were known for hosting. Suddenly, everyone ended up outside, watching or, in the case of us children, crying in horror, as my father screamed in rage at Uncle Gilbert. As my father began choking him, Uncle Gilbert landed one direct, swift kick to my father's groin. My father released his grip, fell to the ground, and groaned in pain. By then, the local police had been called and arrived. Uncle Gilbert and Mom were asked if they wanted to press charges against my father, but they did not. My father crawled into bed shortly after the police left and slept until morning. The incident was never mentioned by anyone, ever. Uncle Gilbert left that same night, and we did not see or hear from him for many years.

But now, on the phone this particular day, his voice was soft and raspy, and he occasionally sounded out of breath. He told me that he was, at that moment, in the hospital but didn't say for what reason. He told me that from his hospital bed, he had just seen me on TV being interviewed and wanted me to know how very proud of me he was for speaking out about my incest experience.

He also asked me to visit him as soon as I could because he had something important he wanted to tell me. A few days later, I visited him in the hospital, and he told me that he, too, as a child, had been sexually assaulted by his older brother Oscar. He said that he had never in his life told anyone about this and that after seeing me speak so courageously about surviving sexual abuse, he now felt he could too. I was shocked and saddened by his revelation but now understood what may have been behind his lifelong battle with various emotional and physical illnesses.

Uncle Gilbert was always referred to as the "sickly" little brother and labeled a hypochondriac for the continuous complaints of aches and pains throughout his life. I later discovered that he also had attempted suicide and suffered from debilitating periods of depression.

When I returned home from my last visit with Uncle Gilbert, I wrote him the following letter, dated September 24, 1988:

Dear Uncle Gilbert,

I truly appreciate your contacting me recently, and I admire the courage it took to call and talk with me about our "history." with your brother. I felt very supported by your call and, at the same time, troubled. Many things have gone through my mind about you and your relationships throughout the Estrada family as a whole, and I can begin to understand now why you are the way you are. This would certainly explain why you've been so physically ill most of your life. I hope this information offers you the support you need at this time. You are not alone anymore! I'll talk with you soon. I love you.

A rare favorite photo with my beloved uncle Gilbert.

As far as I know, he died without ever telling another living soul. I was reminded once again that perpetrators don't usually start or stop victimizing only one person. There were most likely at least one or two other victims before you. The reality of not speaking out about your perpetrator is that he or she will inevitably find more victims after you. Just as surely as family abuse histories continue to prove.

CHAPTER 17

NAMBLA

Unfortunately, there is a segment of our society that condones the sexual abuse of children as positive and of which I strongly disagree. NAMBLA, The North America Man/Boy Love Association, is a world-wide organization of men who firmly believe that it's normal and acceptable for adults to engage in sexual relations with underage boys. They are an extremely well-organized body of predators from all walks of life and all over the world. NAMBLA members maintain local, regional, and state chapters and utilize the Internet to solicit underage victims for sexual contact with its adult members.

In 1999, I had discovered one of NAMBLA's regional leaders operating right in my own backyard. My partner and I were living in the small town of Truth or Consequences in New Mexico, approximately two hours south of Albuquerque. The town is known for both its unusual name and its natural hot springs facilities scattered throughout the town. Over a four-year period, and through a retail business we operated there, we encountered several suspicious residents, including a prominent local artist and his constant companion, Jim.

For some odd reason, the town of Truth or Consequences has, in the four years I lived there, consistently drawn a number of unusual residents. Prominent among them was a publicly "out" gay man named Jim. Jim lived alone in an isolated house right on the river and presented himself in public as an eccentric, well-educated individual. He had a "know it all" type of personality and had an opinion on everything and everyone. Jim's best friend in town, also openly gay, was a commercially successful artist known for both his flower paintings and erotic male nude paintings.

Over the years, I had heard rumors that Jim was attracted to young boys and was known sometimes to have young lovers living with him. I was suspicious of this and maintained my personal distance from him. He and his artist friend were not very approachable and always struck me as suspiciously odd.

One afternoon, a mutual acquaintance of Jim and ours came calling and asking for help. Jim had suddenly been admitted to a hospital for severe depression and placed on suicide watch. Without asking questions, my partner Antonio volunteered to accompany several others from the community to Jim's home to help clean up weeks of accumulated filth. I was not available at the time to participate.

As soon as the group opened the front door, it was apparent that Jim had stopped caring for himself and his home. For many, many months, Jim had spread animal and human feces all over the interior of the house. It was overrun with grotesque garbage, all of which gave off an overwhelming repulsive and overwhelming stench.

They could not walk directly inside because there were no visible pathways through all the debris. The halls and rooms were simply impassable. Jim had been living alone in this mess for weeks during a complete nervous breakdown, and no one knew. The group decided to open all the windows and doors and began hauling trash, piece by piece, to the yards surrounding the house.

During the clean-up, Antonio found boxes of child pornography, sexually explicit photographs of Jim and his artist companion, manuals of how to seduce children, and piles of opened NAMBLA correspondence from all over the country. Antonio knew all about NAMBLA from my work with sexual abuse prevention organizations and began to read over some of the letters. He found letters addressed from NAMBLA's national headquarters, thanking Jim for being the southwest region's main contact and for assisting with the arrangement of acquiring boys for sex from nearby Juarez, Mexico.

Antonio immediately alerted and informed those present, but they each chose to disregard and ignore the graphic evidence before them.

Someone else found a footlocker near Jim's bed which held various types of sexual paraphernalia, including gigantic "sex toys," jars of lubricant, plastic bags, ropes, chains, and handcuffs. Antonio was repulsed and had never before seen such explicit materials on pedophilia, even manuals describing in detail how to seduce boys into sex. Antonio was outraged at the apathy and lack of concern from those present and immediately left the property.

When Antonio returned home, he informed me of everything he had seen regarding Jim's NAMBLA and child pornography materials, and we decided to contact the local police department. Unfortunately, the police told us that they could not do anything because he had entered Jim's home without his expressed permission, even though that entry had been in an emergency situation. The criminal evidence in the home could never be used in court because it was considered illegally obtained. We were stunned, disappointed, and felt our hands were tied.

Our next move was to report this to the FBI, which we did. We were told that for months now, the FBI had an ongoing investigation of Jim and his pedophile activities. The FBI also told us the materials we saw in Jim's home that linked him with NAMBLA could never be used in court as evidence for the same reason the local police had said. Once again, we had hit a block wall.

My partner and I made it known to Jim's artist friend that we knew of his NAMBLA involvement and that we were not going to keep silent. Jim's friend hired a local lawyer and had him confront us in our place of business with the threat of a lawsuit. The attorney demanded that we "cease and desist" from talking about Jim and his NAMBLA connection. We referenced the FBI's working files on Jim's activities, and Antonio promptly escorted this attorney out of our business establishment. From that day on, neither the lawyer nor Jim's friend ever confronted or threatened us again.

After we sold our business property and moved out of Truth or Consequenes, we received information that Jim had moved to San Miguel de Allende in Mexico because he knew the FBI was closing in. His riverside home in Truth or Consequences sat empty for months, if not years.

In March 2003, we learned from reading a newspaper clipping a friend had sent us that Jim had committed suicide outside a public park in Las Cruces, New Mexico. After a police chase, he drove to a public park and took his life with a handgun. Jim's artist friend still lives and paints in his studio home in Truth or Consequences.

This experience with Jim opened my eyes to the sad fact that pedophiles are alive and well within both straight and gay communities. This is a subject many openly gay people appear too uncomfortable even to approach. Without a doubt, the idea of acknowledging gay pedophiles out among the straight community is simply considered by many in the GLBT (Gay, Lesbian, Bisexual, and Transgender) community, too threatening a topic to discuss. Many feel that acknowledging the reality of pedophiles within GLBT communities works against any positive social recognition GLBT communities has made over the past twenty-five years.

I'm here to say that as a gay man and a non-offending adult survivor of sexual abuse, I regrettably acknowledge the fact that gay pedophiles exist and are living within our gay and straight neighborhoods. There are heterosexual pedophiles in the straight population and homosexual pedophiles in the LGBTQ population. Both are serious threats and need to be stopped. To deny this is to set society up for failure in protecting children from all predators.

It is, therefore, my belief that every pedophile (homosexual and heterosexual) must be stopped and prosecuted to the fullest extent of the law. It would be a personal dream of mine to one day witness gay and straight citizens joining together in public to prosecute all child molesters, no matter their sexual orientation, their profession, or how much money they have, because every molester needs to be stopped.

The final point is that we citizens have the right to demand immediate notification by local authorities when convicted sex offenders are present in our neighborhoods. Fortunately, more and more states today are implementing updated sexual predator laws to include stricter monitoring of convicted sexual predators and neighborhood alert campaigns. With the help of many new Internet watch groups, communities have a bit more of a chance to identify potential threats within their neighborhoods. It's not too much to ask to be able to take additional protective measures, based on appropriate information regarding sex offenders and the potential risk they pose to our children's safety and health.

Meltdown

My peace of mind, emotional strength, and optimism for a positive future became seriously and unexpectedly tested one day, in front of a large public audience. Unfortunately, the day-to-day, month-to-month, year-to-year reality of a survivor's life is one of reoccurring emotional, physical, and sexual challenges.

I had spent several years of my newly liberated life busy running the organization for non-offending adult male survivors, writing monthly newsletters, and, from my home, answering phone calls and letters from all over the country, from survivors and professionals in the field of recovery. On occasion, I traveled nationally to present at conferences and was interviewed on various television and radio talk shows. I received awards and acknowledgments from numerous survivor organizations, including a letter of recognition from President George H.W. Bush, and of course it was on official White House stationery.

May 20, 1991

Dear Friends:

Word has reached me of your outstanding record
of community service. I congratulate you on your
achievements.

Many of America's most pressing social problems
can best be solved through a renewal of the values
on which our Nation was founded: duty, acceptance
of personal responsibility, commitment, and a respect
for every individual that expresses itself in direct
or consequential action in behalf of others. Efforts
such as yours are evidence that these values remain
firmly embedded in the American character. I commend
you for making a difference in the life of your
community.

Barbara joins me in wishing you every success as you
continue to set a fine example for your friends and
neighbors. May God bless you.

Sincerely,

George Bush

The Volunteers and Staff of PLEA
356 West Zia Road
Santa Fe, New Mexico 87505

White House Letter

After several intense years of "survivor" work, I began to experience significant emotional burnout that culminated in a psychological
meltdown episode while addressing conference attendees during
one of my presentations. It all came to a dramatic head, just moments

into my presentation before a national survivor conference in San Francisco, California.

As I was speaking, I suddenly lost my ability to focus on what I was saying. I felt that my brain had just died, and words were not coming forth as they had previously in so many lectures in the past. I could not read or understand my own notes; none of the text made any sense to me. I had given this lecture many times before using the exact same notes but could no longer make intellectual connections. I felt immediate anxiety and panic race throughout my body as the audience sat there hanging on the last word I spoke in mid-sentence. I could not move, make a sound, or speak one word. I stood frozen in time, looking down and simply staring at the top of the podium.

I felt my face flush red, and my body tingled with heat as I desperately tried to speak, but my words remained mumbled inside my head. Pressure built up inside my head, and just as I was about to faint, I grabbed onto the podium with both hands and somehow managed to excuse myself. Then I found myself glancing out over the audience and cautiously raised one finger, and gestured just one second.

The audience sat patiently for several awkward moments while my trembling hand lifted a glass of water to my lips and sipped a drink. Now, my mind was racing, and a sudden urge to cry came over me, with tears welling up in my eyes. It took everything inside me to speak up and apologize to the audience. I told them that I was suddenly not feeling well, which was obvious. After several moments of silence from the audience, I asked them if they wouldn't mind if, instead of the formal presentation I had intended, I just answer questions. Fortunately for me, they were accommodating and launched into numerous familiar questions, questions that I, as a survivor, could easily and comfortably answer in my sleep.

I sat surrounded by survivors and professionals who worked with us in an informal circle and answered questions and discussed many common concerns. After the questions ended, I concluded the session by thanking them once again for their understanding. I quickly left the conference, psychologically drained and physically exhausted. On my travel home that night, I decided that, for my own emotional and physical health, I needed to stop my involvement in survivor/abuse work and let others take up the cause. I realized that day that I had been giving much of my personal energy towards other survivors' healing journey and ignoring my own inner self-maintenance. This is easily overlooked by many advocates in the healing and recovery profession and also needs to be better addressed.

I ended my association with all survivor-related organizations, therapists, authors, and related issues; donated the entire remaining inventory of my recovery books to another male survivor organization for free distribution to their members; and disappeared from public survivor recovery life. Fortunately, the initial groundwork for other male survivors and organizations to publicly come forward had been firmly set forth. With more male survivor organizations, conferences, and books being offered as resources, I was relieved and happy to step back to care for.

Occasionally, I would hear about or read something about sexual abuse victims or survivors, but nothing more. I followed the male survivor's movement by visiting websites and browsing the self-help recovery sections of bookstores. I had seen new and revised books by authors Patrick Carnes, Mick Hunter, Mike Lew, Laura Davis, and others, as well as a host of new international male survivor resources. I felt comforted that many male survivors now had access to more resource support than when I first came forward in 1985.

CHAPTER 18

FATHER JOHN RESURFACES

During the early years of our relationship, I introduced my partner Antonio to Father John Raab. Antonio's initial impression of Father John was that he was unexplainably odd and felt uncomfortable in his presence.

Father John tried to befriend Antonio but Antonio's intuition told him to keep his distance. Over these many years, Antonio has been witness to my repeated dealings with Father John, his predatory behavior, his attempts to communicate with me, and the dismissive responses from several representatives from the Claretian Missionary Order and other Catholic Church authorities.

In 2004, nine years after submitting several warning letters to Claretian Fathers Martin and Ferrante, I was again faced with new, disturbing information about Father John, and I was compelled to once again contact Father Ferrante for help. I was introduced to a man who shared with me exact details of his experiences with Father John's sexual advances while attending religious services at a local Catholic Newman Center. Here is yet another letter sent March 16, 2004, to Father Ferrante:

Dear Father Ferrante,

I hope this letter finds you well. Knowing that it has been years since we last spoke in person, I would have preferred to visit with you face to face, but residing in separate states has made this difficult.

Unfortunately, I am once again faced with yet another incident between Father John Raab and a man of whom I recently became aware. This individual claims to have had a similar physical/sexual relationship with Raab, as I reported to both you and Father Martens in January of 1995. Needless to say, I was shocked and surprised to hear about this man's experiences and encounters with Father Raab.

At the time of our correspondence in 1995, I felt you were sincere in your support of my pursuing the significance of what I'd suffered through all those past years. With this letter, I know I can place confidence in your judgment once again. Please contact me at your earliest to discuss this further.

Sincerely,

Hank Estrada

Father Ferrante did eventually contact me by phone and assured me that Father John was no longer in a position of leadership over young men and had been confronted about his past behaviors. Father Ferrante also asked for details about the man who alleged that Father John sexually assaulted him, but I never received any.

At this point, I felt, once again, that I had done all I possibly could to warn those responsible for Father John's future assignments about his sexual predatory history/behavior and pleaded with them to stop him. Is it possible that Father John has never had any intention of addressing his sexual impulses or of seeking appropriate help for his predatory behavior? In my opinion, he should not be permitted to remain a priest, especially one in charge of younger male students.

The documented history of repeated complaints and warnings by even one person over the years should, by now, warrant the immediate suspension of Father John's priestly faculties and permanent removal from the priesthood, but it has not.

Over the years since I first reported Father John, I know that he has served in various communities as a parish priest, teacher, and spiritual director in both the U.S. and overseas. In addition, Father John has previously been assigned to various seminary training programs with other groups of young men, and I can only wonder how many of these have become his silent victims. Unfortunately, only his Claretian superiors with access to his personal file know while the rest of us are simply left to forever wonder.

In the spring of 2005, I was contacted by then Provincial Father Roland Lozano, CMF, asked me for any additional details and identities of other alleged victims of Father John. Father Lozano informed me that Father John was requesting an overseas ministry assignment in Germany, and his personnel records were being investigated prior to acceptance. Father Lozano told me that Father John denies seducing me while we were assigned to Saint Anne's parish in Fort Worth, Texas, and claims that all he did was simply "come out" as a gay man to me and nothing more. Father Lozano claimed to have tracked down the other alleged male victim who supposedly denies anything sexual ever happened between him and Father John while at a Catholic Newman Center in Los Angeles.

I was not surprised to hear this because this alleged victim specifically expressed to me, after describing in familiar detail his physical/sexual encounters with Father John, that he would deny the abuse should he ever be publicly confronted. I informed Father Lozano about this, and the investigation took an abrupt detour.

Father Lozano asked if I would be willing to testify before the Claretian governing board in Germany who were considering hiring Father John and I said yes. He asked if I would permit him to submit all the correspondence I had submitted over the years to the agency and I said most definitely yes.

After several weeks of wondering whether or not I would be summoned or called upon to testify, Father Lozano informed me that Father John's hiring consideration had been withdrawn. I've also, once again, been reassured by Father Lozano that Father John is barred from any further assignments where young men are involved and will not be assigned to any community parish ministries. I remain skeptical, and I pray that this, too, isn't just another disappointing, broken promise whose intent is simply to dismiss and silence me once again.

I have been told repeatedly by Father Lozano that Father John adamantly denies all the allegations of sexual contact between us while we were together during my seminary training. He does continue to admit that the only inappropriate thing he did as my spiritual director and supervisor was simply to confide in me his own gay sexual orientation and nothing more. He is lying.

The continuation of this one false statement by Father John speaks volumes about his moral integrity and lack of personal responsibility for the seriousness of his sexual predatory disposition. It is the single most upsetting lie that compels me now to identify Father John Raab, CMF publicly, and all that has happened. It is because of this one lie Father John insists as his truth that leaves me no other option but to challenge this lie publicly. My only reason for exposing Father John is my desperate attempt to stop him from further victimizations.

Shameful Church

Finally, after years of silence from the church, courageous survivors of clergy sexual abuse have organized together to speak out and fight the hierarchy for ignoring, concealing, and protecting pedophile men among the clergy. We have here yet another instance of "family." type of denial by the church and avoidance of the subject of child sexual molestation. In this case, the "family" is the Roman Catholic Church.

Within the Catholic Church, the issue of the pedophile priest has long been viewed as a serious psychological problem with moral implications: a "problem" that, in their minds, could be corrected with extended periods of rest, private retreats, and spiritual direction.

The church has been determined to work things out within its own structure, not unlike any dysfunctional family with similar issues, and therefore, has seldom sought assistance from professional resources outside its own organization. The church can no longer dismiss the millions of survivors who have bravely come forward if it intends to resolve the crisis it now faces. The countless litigations continue, and lawsuits are successfully being won in favor of sexual abuse survivors.

Unfortunately, the Catholic Church has responded to the seriousness of this moral crisis with inconsistent claims of penance, followed by calculated intimidation tactics against survivors and their families. The church leadership has attempted to detract from its responsibility by focusing media attention on the financial losses it now faces due to endless lawsuits against it. Proclamations and declarations have come out, spouting new policies and procedures regarding the problems of pedophile clergy: what to do with them, how to handle allegations, and finally, offering support and assistance to victims. On paper, these new assertive directives seem to address the problems fairly; however, in reality, so much is left to be desired.

This area of the clergy, priests, in particular, molesting members of their congregation is one that remains foremost in many parishioners' minds. We can't imagine how many victims of clergy sexual abuse are still out there, intimidated and afraid to speak out in our communities. I only know that a tremendous amount of education, action, and healing needs to happen between the leaders of the church, the clergy, and their congregations.

The Catholic Church, in my opinion, has a long, long way to go in rebuilding the faith, trust, and confidence of many of its congregation and for many like myself who don't believe it ever will.

In July of 2007, a statement by Pope Benedict XVI, claiming that "the only true way to salvation is through Catholicism," seemed to undermine years of ecumenical peace and fellowship, not only among non-Catholic organizations but non-Christian ones as well. Pope Benedict's focus on homosexual men in the clergy as the root of the pedophile priest crisis is, likewise, caustic and misguided. Pope Benedict and those who accept his "unholy madness" can only expect to experience further distrust of church authority and even more crime from behind the pulpit.

Because the Catholic Church in some communities continues to behave just like a typical sexual abuse family—with denial, secrecy, and avoidance—it must be intensely watched and challenged so that any sexual predators who remain among the current active clergy the

139

population are caught, identified, and expelled from priesthood and religious life.

Children have always been susceptible to sexual molestation by clergy because parents customarily hold clergy in such high regard. The opportunity for a priest or clergyman to abuse the trust of parents and children has, until recent years, been highly underestimated. What we have now seen happen is that many parents and survivors have come forward to confront the church for its irresponsible policies of protecting known pedophile priests.

By now, we are all familiar with the typical practice of secret re-assignment used to protect sex offenders and their crimes. Just move them secretly out of one parish and into another one. Say nothing to the new parishioners, and everything will work out fine. This has been the practice. Parishes unknowingly receive the newly reassigned priest into their parishes without warning of his abuse history, past accusations, or activity, thus becoming the most likely candidates for victimizations to reoccur.

"But He's a Real Good Man!"

Years after I had left the seminary, I learned that two young priests I knew—one a Claretian priest, Father Lawrence (Larry) Lovell, and the other diocesan priest, Father Theodore (Ted) Llanos — were both charged with numerous sexual assaults of children while serving in assigned parishes.

Father Lovell was completing his studies for the priesthood and was preparing for ordination when I was introduced to him at a Claretian retreat center. Larry, as we were introduced, was a very friendly, outgoing guy who seemed to be looking forward to his ordination and priesthood. He had a witty sense of humor and was often joking around with us younger seminarians. I had talked briefly and socially with Larry during the weekend retreat and found him very pleasant. I lost contact with Larry after his ordination and priestly assignment because I was concentrating on my own seminary studies.

Father Lovell was placed on leave from the Claretian Missionary Order in 1985, and convicted in 1986 for sexual abuse offenses. In

1992 Father Lovell was laicized (formally removed from the Catholic priesthood). He was arrested again in 2003 and convicted of sexual abuses that had occurred while he was a priest between 1970 and 1980. He was sentenced to serve a fourteen-year prison sentence in an Arizona state prison for these crimes.

Remarkably, while attending a dinner together, I heard an unexpected expression of support for Father Lovell by Father Lozano and another former Claretian priest. The former Claretian priest, who had been a classmate of Father Lovell, stated, "But he's a good man," while discussing Father Lovell's prison sentence. Even after a criminal conviction of sexual abuse crimes, Father Lovell's former classmate and Father Lozano felt the need to discount the ugly reality of this convicted sexual predator and defend him as still being "a good man."

Their expression of support for Father Lovell took me completely by surprise because it came from two individuals with master's educations and extensive morals and ethics training. They seemed devoid of anger and disgust regarding Father Lovell's sexual assault crimes and seemed to lack compassion for his victims. It's these unwarranted sentiments of support for sex abuse perpetrators by nonvictims that disturb me the most today. Yes, these perpetrators may have been nice, wonderful people while in your presence but are absolutely unforgivable monsters to those of us who experienced their repeated assaults.

The second sexual predator priest I knew, Father Ted Llanos, was young, friendly, and pleasant in my presence. I had worked around Father Llanos while I was assisting Father Brian Doran and his hearing-impaired ministry at St. Bernard's Parish in Eagle Rock, California. Father Ted was an associate pastor there, and I was impressed at his tremendous artistic talents for liturgy preparations, prayer services, and multi-media presentations. Father Ted not only designed banners to decorate the walls of the church but also did all the sewing of the banners too! He was an extremely talented, energetic, and creative man—a priest I had hoped to be like one day. He always seemed to be smiling, in a good mood, and cracking jokes. He was very likable and easy to approach, and parishioners young and old would flock around him after his liturgies. I admired his enthusiasm and attractive personality. I could have never thought or suspected that he would eventually become known as the #4 pedophile on the Los Angeles Archdiocese list of top ten sexual predators.

The number of victims rose quickly once the authorities publicly presented their case findings. In 1995 over thirty individuals came foreword and accused him of sexual abuse and, in 1997, as the true facts behind his crimes continued to build against him, Father Ted Llanos committed suicide.

I met both men but never suspected something this evil was occurring. The news of their tragic life outcomes saddened and angered me at the same time. My memories of them are forever marked by their criminal predator behavior. It saddens me to think now how much damage the church leaders might have prevented had they made the moral decision to stop these offenders as soon as reported. Unfortunately, in these two cases, we will never know.

Sadly, since the initial printing of UnHoly Communion, I've been shocked and deeply disappointed to learn of other former Claretian associates I knew, that have been exposed regarding their own histories of sexual assaults while serving as active clergymen in Claretian parish ministries. Fr. William "Bill" Paiz, Brother Richard Suttle and Brother Modesto Leon have each been added to the growing list of clergy perpetrators.

In April 2011, I also received the following email from the then, newly Assigned Provincial Superior of the Claretian Missionary Order, Father Rosendo Urrabazo referencing Fr. Raab. Clearly, there remained serious concerns regarding Fr. Raab that prompted the following email request.

Dear Mr. Estrada:

My name is Fr. Rosendo Urrabazo, CMF and I am the new provincial of the Claretian Missionaries here in the US. I have tried to call you, but the number I have from 2004 is not in service.

I am doing an investigation regarding Fr. John Raab and would like to talk with you about your past letters and email communications.

Please call me at my cell number or send me a number where I can reach you.

Thank you for your help in this matter.

Rosendo Urrabazo, CMF

Provincial Superior

Claretian Missionaries - USA Province

I chose to ignore this request because I had lost all trust in this organization. The continued false expressions of sincerity, compassionate concern and lack of moral responsibility to end repeated victimizations by a known sexual predator was why I did not respond. This religious organization, one of many, along with the larger Catholic Church has relied heavily on clergy abuse victims accepting monetary compensation settlements in return for their silence.

I'm asking survivors not to trust Catholic Church leadership to stand up for survivors, to help us receive justice or to permanently cast out known sexual predator clergy. It is not enough to simply remove predators from public ministry or assign them to a solitary desk job, they must be held socially accountable and criminally prosecuted.

Father Rosendo's Failed Leadership Exposed

The following examples of moral irresponsibility and deliberate deceit by religious superiors upon the public regarding the handling of exposed predator clergy is most evident in Fr. Rosendo's words and actions here.

Sometime in 2008, the Claretian Missionaries (CMF) of the U.S. Western Province notified the Diocese of Phoenix that they had reviewed a credible report of sexual abuse of a minor against Bro. Richard Suttle, CMF. In that report, Bro. Richard Suttle is accused of engaging in sexual abuse of a minor during the 1982-83 school year while at Sacred Heart School in Prescott, where Bro. Suttle was a teacher and a coach. Bro. Suttle was also employed at Bourgade Catholic High School in Phoenix from 1988 to 1998 and served as principal of Sacred Heart School between 2006 and 2008.

Damage control protocol by the Church or, as in this case, the Claretian Missionary Order immediately initiates a public proclamation stating they have removed the accused from any ministry involving minors, will restrict and monitor his movements and will not reassign this individual to the diocese.

As regularly happens in the majority of these instances, the accused is relocated to another community with absolutely no advance public warning. Clearly an inexcusable attempt to cover up their failure to protect the public from further assaults.

In December of 2010, Bro. Suttle was assigned to East Nigeria Province as part of a team to begin a mission in the English-speaking part of Cameroon. Bro. Suttle was to become the manager of three schools and director of children and youth choirs. Claretian documents also report that Bro. Suttle repeated his youth leadership role in a new Vietnam mission and was then selected to direct the Nigerian Claret Secondary School, Nekede.

In 2013, a news investigation reported that Bro. Suttle was sent to Argentina by Fr. Rosendo Urrabazo, CMF, at the same time, a victim's advocacy group, criticized the Order for allowing Suttle to remain in the ministry. Fr. Urrabazo has repeatedly stated that Bro. Richard had been removed from any ministry with children and assigned internal work for the Order. Clearly, that was never the case.

In April of 2005, I received the following e-mail from Father Roland Lozano, CMF the Provincial of the Claretian Order in that year, indicating that he was aware of my work with sexual abuse survivors stating: "Thank you for the courage you have so faithfully shown over the years. I am very proud of you and all the efforts you are making to protect young people—and everyone—from abuse."

Since that dinner, I had with Father Lozano and the former Claretian Priest who expressed support for Larry Lovell, I have come to treat these types of seemingly heartfelt messages as superficial and with great suspicion and distrust.

I believe that the Catholic Church, the clergy, and other leaders of organized religion's must demand themselves a higher level of courage to openly discuss sexual abuse, pedophilia, victim outreach, adult survivor issues, and prevention strategies. They must actively seek out professionals in the prevention and recovery fields, specifically from outside the confines of the church, and their exclusively private circle of resources, and provide honest updated workshops, lectures, and educational programs for members of the congregations and clergy.

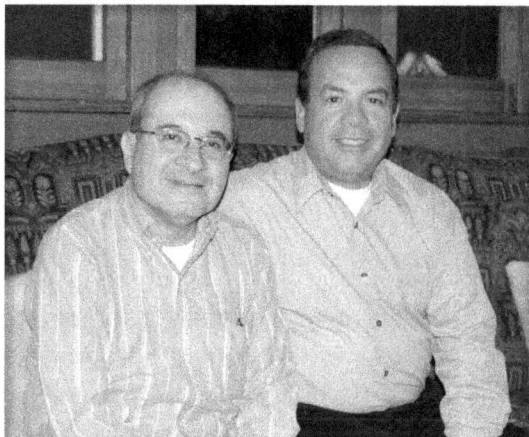

Father Lozano and I, the evening "but he's a good man." the comment was made.

Those members of the clergy with known histories of pedophilia MUST BE PERMANENTLY REMOVED from their positions and barred from ministries that provide potential opportunities for victim assaults. They must never be reassigned to a similar ministry or communities where contact with children and young adults is inevitable.

In April of 2007, Pope Benedict XVI declared a statement that any Catholic politician who openly supports legislation in favor of abortion rights shall be excommunicated immediately from the Catholic

Church. Most Catholics understand that this is a very grave and unforgiving punishment for such controversial thinking or behavior. Why then has Pope Benedict, or any Pope, NOT declared immediate Excommunication upon every single pedophile priest and Catholic sexual predator found guilty of these crimes?! Are sexual predators and pedophile clergy above ex-communication? I think not.

Sexual predators and pedophile clergy should be excommunicated without hesitation as soon as the allegations are proven true. Their behavior is immoral, reprehensible and they should be immediately expelled from the priesthood, religious life, and the Catholic religion. Members of the congregation should insist that their church improve and provide sexual abuse awareness, prevention, and intervention programs. Again, children need to be taught the difference between appropriate and inappropriate touching, even if it's their priest doing the touching. They must be encouraged to foster their own sense of self-respect at as early an age as possible by not allowing anyone to explore or violate their bodies secretly.

Further, if any uncomfortable touching occurs, the child needs to be taught that telling others right away is the first thing to do towards getting the inappropriate behavior stopped.

Appropriately trained religious leaders, together with qualified sex abuse professionals, have to be given the opportunity to facilitate community discussions on child sexual abuse prevention for both clergy and non-clergy. Foremost, and not to be ignored, is to include the topic of sexual victimization by clergy and how to address the subject with children. Simply avoiding or ignoring the topic will only increase the odds of it happening.

If church authorities and representatives were to initiate honest awareness/prevention programs about child sexual abuse with congregation members, I believe that those clergy currently molesting children would stop for fear of being discovered, exposed, and prosecuted. I believe that if Pope Benedict declared that all known sexual predators and pedophiles would receive immediate ex-communication, further sexual victimizations by clergy could surely be prevented.

Secondly, parishioners should be better prepared to report suspicious or alleged incidents of clergy sexual behavior to civil authorities first, then to the religious authorities of the church organization itself. The church leadership should never be the first party contacted when sexual abuse behavior is suspected or alleged, but instead, one should go directly to civil authorities.

Lastly, immediate and appropriate actions must be taken to offer free professional "non-denominational" counseling to those clergy abuse survivors who want this for as long as is necessary. And perpetrators must be assigned on-going mandatory therapy and permanently removed from ministries where access to potential victims is greatest.

In 2020, a new Associated Press (AP) investigation found that almost 1,700 Catholic priests and staff accused of child abuse live freely in the US, with no oversight from law enforcement or church supervision. The AP found that since they were accused, 65 have been charged with a variety of crimes, 76 have licenses to work in schools or medical establishments, and only 85 charged with sex crimes are registered sex offenders. More than 130 dioceses in the US have publicly named priests, deacons, monks, and worshippers accused of historic child abuse since August 2018. The discovery was part of a broader investigation into the whereabouts of 5,100 priests, deacons, monks, and laypeople in Roman Catholic Churches in the US "credibly" accused of child sexual abuse dating back decades.

CHAPTER 19

CHURCH WATCHDOGS

Each one of us must each keep a close watch on Catholic Church leaders, both old and new, their declarations, practices, and approaches to offering assistance to victims and, in particular, any new abuse reporting procedures they are instructing their parishioners to follow. Catholic Church officials continue to prove that they still cannot be fully trusted, and make weak, selective attempts to demonstrate their commitment to end clergy sexual abuse.

Since the clergy abuse crisis first came into the public's awareness, victim advocates and legal professionals representing victims have expressed that the church hierarchy has acted like organized crime without heartfelt apologies or sympathy for survivors. Unfortunately, it is difficult to dispute the perception of the Catholic Church parading itself as a morally superior, untouchable religious institution when it, more often than not, acts like organized crime in its attempts to pacify and silence clergy abuse survivors and their families.

Not only have I experienced this treatment firsthand with the Claretian Missionary Order and Father John Raab's superiors, but I am also sad to say that these activities continue today in religious communities throughout the world. The Catholic Church's arrogant hierarchy of power has produced a significant number of "Tony Soprano" type priests, bishops, and cardinals who will say and do anything to shame and intimidate former victims from seeking justice.Survivors have been strong-armed and bullied by church officials into settling their grievances against the diocese with specific, long-term behavioral requirements and outrageous conditions of silence.

National Catholic rehabilitation center for pedophile clergy located in Jemez Springs, New Mexico, now defunct.

For several years now, hardball defense tactics were commonplace all over the country since the sex abuse scandal erupted in 2002. Through intense public outrage and survivor advocacy support organizations, bishops were forced to drop these tactics. However, as the media focus lessens, some old-timer Catholic officials simply refuse to change and are returning to earlier intimidation tactics. For these unfortunate souls, it appears to be Catholic religious business as usual.

Clergy sex abuse survivors have been, and continue to be, re-victimized by Catholic clergy leaders, diocesan representatives, and church lawyers. There remain prominent, powerful church representatives, who continue to condone the actions of silent conspirators, specifically, those who keep perpetrator histories of sexual misconduct by clergy from parishioners and communities.

In January 2006, an article was published in the Miami Herald, describing that the Archdiocese of Miami initially extended "pastoral concern" and "prayers" for the alleged victim and his family when one of its priests was legally charged with sexual abuse. Several days later, after the priest was officially arrested, the archdiocese took a much less sympathetic position and replied, "his (the victim's) own negligence" was to blame for what the priest allegedly did to him as a ten-year-old boy. I have to ask now, in this day and age, with all that's been said and promised by the Catholic Church, just how incredibly outrageous and nasty does this published response sound to you? The reality is there are still many practicing Catholics who I would like to believe this is the case.

On top of this and according to civil, criminal, and archdiocesan records, this particular predator priest had already been reported on since the late 1970s. Confidential church records also indicate other alleged victims of this priest came forward to express in identical detail how they, too, were sedated and repeatedly sodomized.

From now on, we must remain suspicious when anyone, a clergy member especially seems to prefer to spend more personal time alone with a child, rather than with other adults or seems interested in pursuing an exclusive relationship with that child. Today's society has earned the right to question and be suspicious of adults who interact exclusively with children.

I also share the opinion of those who say that large "nonprofit." charitable organizations like the Catholic church should have the tax-exemption status revoked under state "racketeering" statutes for all the years of consciously conspiring to conceal the criminal activities and records of sexual predator priests. Perhaps the loss of the nonprofit status is what should happen to all nonprofit religious organizations and institutions that protect sexual predator members.

This is what legally happens to any other legal operation or business that conspires to break the laws by protecting criminals, obstructing justice, and implementing intimidation tactics against citizens who expose their crimes.

The Catholic Church leadership continues to act like an out of control dysfunctional family: hiding behind secrets and covering up sexual violations of innocent citizens, ignoring the perpetrator's likelihood to assault again, and portraying everyday parish life as normal, peaceful, and righteous.

Religious leaders who react arrogantly toward survivors who seek their assistance, naively hope that by periodically proclaiming a moral decree about something completely unrelated to the clergy sexual abuse subject, parishioners will remain distracted from understanding their spiritual leaders' true positions.

I am making it my personal mission to expose these individuals and their tactics of distraction whenever discovered and, in the now-familiar words of a popular CNN news anchor, I will be "keeping them honest!"

The institution of the Catholic Church, including its leaders, has become for me yet another sexually abusive family entity that, instead of inspiring love, loyalty, trust, and faith has instilled in many a deep sense of despair, shame, and contempt the likes of which we may never overcome or recover from.

Andrew & Jason

Although I never expected to become a serious predator watchdog, I have found great satisfaction in meeting other survivors who have committed to following the lives of their perpetrators. In 2018 two such exceptional survivors, Jason and Andrew unexpectedly entered my life, and we banded together to successfully stop the parole release of convicted sex offender Larry Lovell.

In February of 2018, I attended a SNAP support meeting in Albuquerque, NM. It had been years since I participated in any survivor support group or meeting , but I decided to offer whatever help I could to the organizers. There were about a dozen attendees, mixed men and women, and during the individual introductions, one male survivor experience caught my attention. It was Jason who told us that his perpetrator was a former Catholic priest. The meeting did not provide much individual socializing but offered plenty of information and food for thought.

As I was out in the parking lot, preparing to drive away, I noticed Jason walking nearby towards his vehicle. I had carried copies of my book and offered him a copy along with my business card. He was not from the area and had about a two and half hour drive home ahead of him. We said goodnight and invited each other to stay in touch.

The next afternoon, I received the following email; "Hi, I'm Jason. We met at the meeting. I'm reading your book, and it's really intense because the same schools you're mentioning in your book are the same schools my perpetrator, Lawrence (Larry) J. Lovell, a former Claretian priest, also attended." I could not believe it. I immediately contacted Jason, and we spoke on the phone for over an hour. I shared my seminary memories of Larry when he and I were students in the seminary together. I recalled Larry as an intelligent, sensitive, and caring individual, not at all like Jason's memories of Larry's grooming and repeated sexual assaults.

Also, in February 2018, Andrew from Arizona emailed me expressing his appreciation for my book and sharing that he was the sole survivor who successfully testified against Larry Lovell in court, which led to Larry's conviction and ultimate prison sentence. I had not ever heard of, or know, any details of Larry Lovell other than the fact that he had left the priesthood, the Claretian Order, and was sentenced to an Arizona prison for sexual molestation of children. I was absolutely amazed by Andrew's heart-wrenching and inspiring story. I offered him my sincere admiration and support for whatever he might face in the future on his continued healing journey.

For the next two years, I remained in phone contact with both Jason and Andrew. On one occasion, while I was traveling through Arizona on business, Andrew and I met for lunch. Although our visit was brief, I left wishing we both lived closer so that face-to-face conversations could happen more.

In January of 2020, I received the following email from Andrew, "Hi Hank, hope the new year is off to a good start! I want to let you know that I received a letter from Arizona Board of Executive Clemency stating that Larry Lovell is going to have a parole hearing on February 11 in Phoenix. Not sure if you are interested in writing to them or being at the hearing, or if you are still in touch with Jason and want to let him know. They notified me as a victim, but anyone can submit letters or attend the hearings. Let me know if you want any more info, and I'll pass it along."

I had never in my life been this close to a fellow survivor who had this opportunity to speak up against his perpetrator and to stop his parole release. None of my perpetrators were ever arrested, prosecuted, or convicted, and I was only able to report them to various individuals without any consequence to my perpetrators.

In February 2020, Andrew and Jason emailed me rough drafts of their statements for review to block Lovell's early parole release and invited my feedback. After making several edits and content suggestions, both statements were submitted to the parole board. Lovell's parole was unanimously denied. In May 2021, Lovell, 73, was released permanently from prison, and a sex offender registry indicates he is now living in Phoenix, Arizona.

Lawrence Lovell

Dysfunctional Family

After years of feeling frustrated by my family's denial and continued silence over my traumatic childhood, I decided to channel my energy into writing a book. Soon after I publicly spoke out about Uncle Oscar's assaults, I was made to feel as though I were the cause because I had admitted participating in sex with him. I felt helpless because I could not trust those family members who should have protected me and who made it very clear that talking about the topics of sex and sexual behavior was unacceptable. No one ever wanted to discuss the subject.

Once the local youth and family services representatives had completed their investigation between my family and me, the situation was never discussed again. I was once more forced to remain silent about my experiences, and for the longest time, I felt completely isolated. My parents and family avoided me and never once brought the subject up again. I expect this shameful silence will recur as a result of this book.

It took me years struggling to learn that most family members who remained silent, including my own father, had themselves been victims of alcoholism and some form of child abuse. I had guessed that these older relatives were too wounded and scared themselves to help me because they never confronted their own painful childhood traumas.

My anger and frustration turned to sorrow for them because they were never given the opportunity to seek help. They spent the majority of their adult lives in silent pain and sorrow: abusing alcohol and drugs, committing physical violence, and possibly engaging in criminal activities. My anger returned once again when I took it upon myself to search out and suggest recovery resources to these family members, but they chose not to pursue my recommendations.

At this point, I realized that I could not help people who did not think they needed help, nor could I convince them otherwise. I quickly realized that I needed to focus my energy on myself. I needed to help myself first before I could attempt to help anyone else. I made the decision to "let go" of my family's baggage and their mental health issues, and I stopped getting caught up in their complaints about the "family problems" they faced. My feeling was that we were now all adults, but they did not want my help. They could not even admit there were serious problems that needed to be addressed, so I chose to separate myself from them. I then became determined to do everything I could, including speaking out publicly, to prevent further family sexual secrets from devouring other children in our family. It didn't stop all the abuse, but it did force some to change their thinking and be more responsible with their own families.

So much energy is spent sorting out family problems that inevitably resurface time and time again. It remains a vicious cycle we often find ourselves combating when unresolved family issues are denied and ignored. It's so damn easy to get caught up in these cycles and let ourselves feel guilty for not helping those in crisis. The problem with this is that these family members will always be "in crisis" and more than likely will continue rehashing the same problems over and over again.

The best advice I can give is to put yourself first. All families experience various stages of healthy and unhealthy, positive and negative interpersonal relationship dynamics, but ultimately you're left with only yourself no matter what; so you, not your family, should be your number one priority. Most dysfunctional family relationships and environments remain the biggest detriment to a survivor's own healing and recovery. As adult survivors, it is our personal responsibility to keep ourselves emotionally healthy, spiritually strong, and psychologically confident, and we can no longer afford to let desperate family drama destroy the positive energy we work so hard to create and maintain.

When it comes to dealing with the stress and anxiety of attending family holidays and celebrations, I've made it a point to avoid those individuals and situations that make me personally uncomfortable. I have learned the hard way that it serves absolutely no purpose for me to suffer in silence at the awkwardness of dealing with dysfunctional and unhealthy family members. I often found that after I leave a family gathering; I am left feeling irritated, annoyed, and upset instead of relaxed and happy. I'm left feeling compromised and emotionally drained after hours of maintaining an artificial grin and superficial conversation. I don't do this anymore, and this has contributed greatly to my personal, ongoing sense of well-being and happiness.

From the survivor's viewpoint, in these types of situations, you are not in a healthy or supportive environment. A majority of our relatives have decided to stay in their own uncomfortable but protective world of denial. Being around these relatives makes you feel stuck in distrust, pain, and anger. More often than not, it becomes easier with time to learn to trust complete strangers, to develop mutual respect with non-family members, which for many, leads to unconditionally loving and supportive relationships. These newfound friends often become the source of new "family" in place of the biological one you had to give up. Similarly, for those who miss their church communities, developing regular contact with a positive spiritual individual and prayer group may help to temporarily replace the spiritual damage and loss of contact with a former religious church family that chose to protect its own interests instead of those of their faithful community members.

You can now choose the "family" environment you want to visit or be in during special celebrations. You choose only those social gatherings which you feel are healthy and emotionally non-threatening. Life is too short of having to endure the painful memories experienced at dysfunctional family gatherings. It's better, whenever possible, to spend as much time as you can around positive, supportive, and understanding people during significant life celebrations and annual holiday gatherings.

Christmas and New Year holidays for me as a child were often periods of great stress and trauma due to the emotional and physical violence I experienced. Today with my life partner, cherished friends, and business associates, these celebrations replace those nightmarish childhood holidays with joyful, special memories. Over the years, I have also attempted to attend Mass during the Christmas season, both in the United States and in other countries, but each time I left feeling uninspired, saddened, and very discouraged. I know there are priests out there who can preach inspiring messages of hope, love, and faith, but I have not experienced one in years. I have read news articles that enrollments in Catholic seminaries continue to drop significantly here in the US and have increased in third world African, South American, and Asian countries.

The new priests of these countries are exclusively instructed and ordained in traditional, conservative Catholic theology, then transferred to staff parishes in the US, where they preach conservatively as they were trained. The liturgies to me feel purely "staged" during the sermons delivered often seem void of any message of hope, inspiration, or relevance for the real-life and times of people today.

My advice, though easier said than done, is to stop putting your family's religious expectations or sense of obligations first. Instead, start surrounding yourself with healthier, spiritually grounded, and positive people. Your happiness and health must take precedence. You deserve it! We survivors need to take much better care of ourselves or at least practice better ways of caring for ourselves.

One of the more difficult tasks in focusing on our happiness is overcoming the feelings of guilt and responsibility towards our family and church communities. There came the point for me when I had done all that I could to help each member of my family, but without success. I had to let go of my false sense of family and get on with my life.

Similarly, the confrontations with Father John Raab and other church clergy also needed to stop because I had said all that was needed to be said. The responsibility has appropriately shifted to where and with whom this needs to be. The weight is lifted, and I no longer feel that my presence at family gatherings or religious church services remained necessary to ensure other people's happiness or approval.

I gained a tremendous sense of self-respect and confidence by deciding not to participate in events that felt emotionally unhealthy and painfully unreasonable. Now I have control of how and with whom I spend my time. There simply is no more room for compromise or self-sacrifice.

I now control how and with whom I spend my free time. It's been extremely liberating.

CHAPTER 20

FINDING HELP

The following are some suggestions on how to get help and support for men who were abused as boys. Men need to be aware that recovery from childhood abuse is possible. An individual begins the process of healing by FIRST AND FOREMOST breaking his silence and talking about his abuse experience. It is important to engage in therapy on a regular basis to deal specifically with the overwhelming psychological and physical trauma created by the abuse.

The next step is to share your experience with other survivors through self-help, therapy, and support groups. In addition, I strongly recommend that survivors read books and other literature about recovery from childhood abuse. Many outline the recovery process to help survivors understand it. If you currently have a drug or alcohol dependency or compulsive behavior problems like sex, eating, gambling, et cetera, these addictions need to be identified and controlled before the sexual abuse recovery process can begin.

These addictive behaviors are serious obstacles to recovery that impact the outcome of physical and emotional change and healing. There is no single healing approach or guideline to follow in order to experience healing. The needs and capabilities of each individual will dictate the approach he will find most comfortable with. I often tell survivors: You are now the only one in control of how your recovery process is going to proceed. You decide at what pace to proceed.

If you have not told anyone about your abuse, find someone you trust and tell them. The more people you tell, the more you'll be able to lessen those feelings of shame and guilt. If you have told someone, and their reaction was not what you had hoped for, don't give up! Continue to seek support, and eventually, you will find that one person who will make all the difference.

Survivor Beware!

It may take you a few attempts at choosing a professional counselor that you feel comfortable speaking with; this process alone can be challenging in itself. However, let me share my first experience with a "professional" counselor that could have ended my willingness to seek help after a disastrous first session. It was just around the time I had contemplated suicide and was desperate for help. I found a "self-pay" crisis and counseling center in the phone book and made an appointment to talk with a counselor.

After I had signed in with the receptionist and waited for a few minutes, my name was called, and I followed the person into a private room. There were three love seats in the middle of the room, facing a wall of large windows. I noticed a toy chest of various plush animals, pillows, and dolls piled off to the side of one of the love seats.

A young woman entered the room right behind me. I did not notice her when I walked into the room until she introduced herself and invited me to sit across from her. She asked me to tell her what had brought me to the clinic today. I briefly told her that I was feeling depressed and had stopped eating and sleeping. She began to ask specific questions, which eventually led to my disclosing that I had been having sex with an older alcoholic man (I did not tell her it was my uncle). She seemed unusually calm about this revelation and said she wanted to try out a new healing "technique" that might help me to get better in touch with my emotions. Keep in mind; this was the very first time I had ever met or seen a therapist of any kind.

She asked me to sit down on the floor directly across from her. She grabbed a soft, plush forest green pillow off the love seat and set it in front of me. She told me to stare at the pillow and to imagine this was the older man I was having sex with. I did not know how this was helping but did as she directed. As I stared at the pillow, the counselor spoke in a soft voice and asked me to recall the last time I had been assaulted and what I was feeling. As I began to feel anger rising within me, she sensed that she was getting somewhere with me and proceeded to say that this pillow before me was my perpetrator and that I should "tell him how [I] feel" right now. My emotions surfaced, and anger erupted as never before.

At that moment, I vaguely remember ripping the pillow into pieces causing stuffing and material to fly throughout the room. I screamed and proceeded to rip apart the already tattered pieces of the pillow. I experienced a complete full-blown rage, and it scared the crap out of not only me but also the therapist. This was the first and only time I had ever permitted myself to get in touch with this level of personal rage. I felt murderous hate overflowing from deep inside me. It terrified me because I had never experienced this before, and here it all was, in an instant, with nowhere to go. I felt physically sick and nearly threw up on myself, and it was totally terrifying. I felt unable to control this anger, which was what shocked me the most, even then. The therapist herself had never dealt with this type of intense, extreme reaction either. This exercise was something she obviously learned in a classroom setting but never actually demonstrated with a person in crisis. She was so horrified that she jumped back, stood up, and ran out of the room. She did not know what to do or how to regain control and left me alone in the room while she went to find help.

Several other people entered the room, her supervisor among them, and they calmed me down. I was exhausted from experience and humiliated for acting like this but did not understand what had just happened. I never returned to that clinic and didn't know what happened to that counselor who, I later found out, happened to be an intern in training.

As a survivor, my biggest challenge remains in not permitting the emotional scars of abuse to obscure my ability to stay focused and rational in my thoughts and behavior. Not to let myself fall into an emotionally paralyzing state of "victim," which I'm sure you survivors know exactly what I mean. I remain very much encouraged by the calls, letters, and e-mails I receive from thousands of survivors throughout the country who have come forward to express their own daily challenges and successes towards recovery and healing.

Despite my sometimes feelings of overwhelming worthlessness, I am grateful and proud to have been able to move through the sadness. I remain emotionally grounded, hopeful, energized, and passionately in love. Understand that through the shared courage of other survivors and despite seemingly endless denials by perpetrators and their supporters, I'm once again able to step up to a new challenge and tell these truths.

S.N.A.P.

After repeatedly disclosing everything that Father John Raab had done over the past few years, I found myself without emotional support resources to get over the disappointments and lack of resolve. I remember hearing about the group of clergy abuse survivors from Boston had formed a nonprofit group but didn't know the name.

After a few moments of surfing on the Internet, I found SNAP (Survivors Network of those Abused by Priests) website. SNAP is a volunteer, nonprofit self-help organization of survivors of clergy sexual abuse and their supporters. I read everything I could on the website and noticed information about an upcoming conference. When I clicked on the conference button, I read that the conference was to be held in Denver, Colorado, within a few weeks. I decided this was a good opportunity to meet the organization and find out what exactly they were doing.

I really couldn't afford a plane ticket at that time, so I purchased a roundtrip bus ticket to Denver from southwest New Mexico, where I lived at the time. It was a very, very long, and uncomfortable thirteen-hour ride. I had managed to find a reasonable hotel room online, about four blocks away from the conference hotel. I arrived at 7 a.m. on the first day of the conference, which was to open at 5 p.m. that evening. I was lucky enough to be allowed into a clean, vacant room before all the checkouts were done. I immediately dropped onto the bed and slept for several hours, despite my excitement and anxiousness about attending the conference. I had not attended a "survivor" conference of any type since the "meltdown" I experienced in July

1997 in San Francisco. To my great surprise, I was welcomed, encouraged, and supported by everyone I met, including the organizers.

I attended as many workshops and presentations as I could and talked with many clergy abuse survivors from all over the country. I was able to share my experiences and challenges with Father John from the beginning right up to the present. I was relieved to have so much support, understanding, and acceptance from this conference experience that, after I returned home, I volunteered to sign on as a SNAP regional representative for the southwest corner of New Mexico.

I was provided with a comprehensive "leaders" manual and quickly dove into organizing. Using the instructions in the leaders manual, I drafted a news release announcing the establishment of a SNAP resource in my hometown. I sent it to every media source I could identify. My news release was printed, and I anticipated at least a few calls. I received one call from a woman whose husband had survived clergy sexual abuse, wanting to know what I had to offer. I explained to her that I was alone in this and sent the news release to see if there were others with similar needs for support. She was the only person in three months of advertising who took the time to respond or inquire.

The woman told me that her husband had not read the news release, and she did not know how he would react to it. She said that he had never talked to a professional therapist about it and felt it best to leave it in the past and move on. I could hear in her voice that she felt differently about this and wished her husband would talk with me. I told her I would be glad to at any time, should he ever feel like talking. I never heard back from her again.

The second and final thing I did as a SNAP representative was to sign up for a free workshop on preventing sexual abuse, sponsored by the Diocese of Las Cruces in New Mexico, which governed over my community. Unfortunately, because of the remoteness and isolation of the small rural community, I was living in, the National SNAP leadership only provided me with a huge start-up manual of how to run a local SNAP organization and conduct meetings. I realized then that I was now completely on my own and without supportive communication with SNAP's national headquarters or official representatives that I had experienced at the conference. A disappointment indeed, but not a deterrent.

A few days later, I learned about a regional training session being offered by the local Catholic diocese and chose to investigate. I admit I was curious to know what the local diocese was now teaching regarding sexual abuse prevention, and if they were going to address sexual predator clergy, specifically with those of us in attendance.

I arrived at a small community parish hall and was amazed to see over one hundred people lined up to register for the workshop. I was told that the diocese encouraged anyone working within the Catholic Church on every level, from clergy to janitor, to attend.

The all-day workshop had two representatives: a spokeswoman from outside the church who was employed by a sexual assault prevention organization and the other, a representative from the Las Cruces diocese. Throughout the day, they covered all the basics of what to look for, spotting behavioral changes, and how to help victims. It was informative and well presented.

Towards the very end of the workshop, when the time had run out, they read quickly through a document they had handed out about reporting suspected sexual abuse. There were a lot of technical and detailed instructions on what the church was responsible for and what it would do to assist victims. The presenters told us that they didn't have time to go over everything in the document but that we should read through it when we had more time.

The last and most interesting point was to report suspected abuse to church "officials" first. It was emphasized that if you suspect or even witness sexual abuse occurring, you are to report it to local church officials first, ignoring a nationwide revised policy that suspected incidents should first be reported to civil authorities, then church representatives. I was disappointed to hear this and thought this was just another diocese's attempt to police itself. After everything the church has promised to do regarding the protection of children, there are still communities being given bad advice. It is in these instances that we must continue to challenge local religious clergy who choose not to follow appropriate legal directives from senior church officials.

Chapter 21

Wolves in Sheep Skins

Not all national "survivor" organizations operate in the survivor's best interest and should not be blindly accepted simply because they have been operating for years. I have experienced several disappointing interactions with two such organizations that I've never shared until this update. I firmly believe that I am not alone in my experiences and hope this chapter will encourage more transparent discussions about how these sensitive situations can best be addressed and confronted.

In September 2012, I was a guest presenter at the (IVAT) 17th International Conference on Violence, Abuse, and Trauma held at the Town & Country Resort & Convention Center in San Diego, CA. My presentation was entitled Male Sexual Victimization - Speaking the Unspeakable.

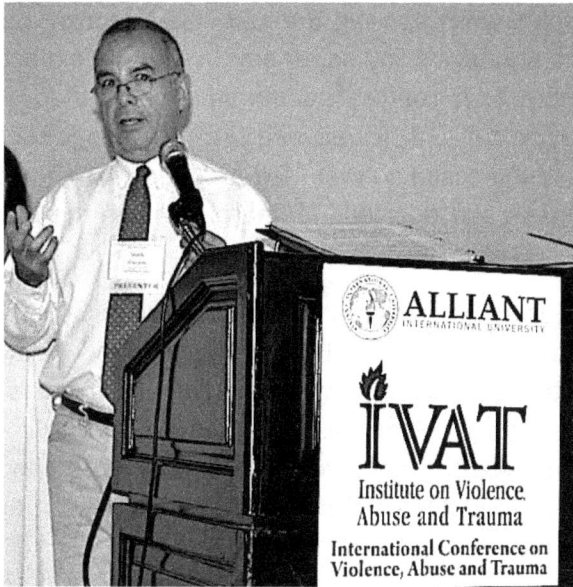

IVAT Conference Presenter

There were many internationally known authors and organizations in attendance, including representatives from the Male Survivor organization. At one point during the first few hours of the conference, I was introduced to Samuel by the Executive Director of Male Survivor. Samuel was very animated and engaging in our first introduction. I was given the impression that Samuel was a regular, popular contributing supporter and advocate of the Male Survivor organization. Our meeting was brief, and we soon went our separate ways after this introduction.

Throughout the day, I would run into Samuel, and we briefly chatted as we passed each other. At one point, during a break, Samuel and I were able to speak a little longer and I found out that he was not a sexual abuse survivor but was attending to be of help and support to the organizers. Samuel asked me what brought me to the conference, and I told him I was presenting. He complimented me on my courage to speak publicly about my assault trauma and healing journey experiences. From then on and throughout the remainder of that day, every time Samuel saw me, he would comment on how special a man I was and how much he admired me.

At one point, while passing Samuel, reached over, patted me on my back, and squeezed my upper arm. I was not expecting this but chose to ignore it. In the proceeding time we met up, Samuel told me that I was a "cutie," followed with "You are soooooooooo beautiful." It was in this instance that I felt an overwhelming sense of uncomfortableness and decided to share this with the Male Survivor Executive Director.

His initial response was that of surprise and disbelief, followed by the statement, "I know Samuel, he wouldn't do this." His suggestion was for me to speak directly with Samuel and express how I was feeling. I felt the Director was equally uncomfortable confronting Samuel did not want to get involved and was more concerned with maintaining his long time "business" association with Samuel rather than supporting me.

I avoided both Samuel and this Director for the remainder of the conference and confronted them both with the following email:

"Dear Samuel,

I'm writing to detail how uncomfortable I felt meeting you at the IVAT Conference this week and want to address why:

You disclosed to me that you were not a "survivor" but had been working for years among us. I assumed you would know how to interact in a more sensitive and professional manner when speaking to a sexual assault survivor like myself. I am compelled to describe what specific things you said and did during our brief interactions, which for sexual assault survivors are highly inappropriate and re-traumatizing. I'd like to believe that this was not your intent and that you will remember these specific points from here forward when first meeting and interacting with survivors.

First, without knowing me or my trauma history, you embraced me upon our first meeting- my perpetrators also embraced and assaulted me without EVER asking. Second, you spoke intimately about your family experience regarding love, being loved and stated you "loved." everyone, "straight, gay, bisexuals too." My perpetrators always spoke of love and what love was, what love should be, and ultimately-SHOWED me what love felt like by repeatedly assaulting me. Third, you said you "thought there was something special about me that you liked" - both perpetrators OFTEN said this as they were repeatedly assaulting me. Fourth, when I passed you, you reached out to touch me and said, "You're a cutie." I did not take this as a compliment but as overt sexual interest in me. This was extremely uncomfortable, and it was entirely inappropriate—gay, straight, or bi. Fifth, you sent me a Facebook message after I returned home saying, "I LOVED meeting you." along with "You are soooooooo Beautiful" - BOTH perpetrators also repeatedly expressed these EXACT statements during their sexual assaults upon me.

This is totally inappropriate adult behavior. You know nothing about me, and there was nothing I said or did that warranted this kind of attention. You were totally out of line. Finally, you expressed, "You're always invited to our house" I felt awkward. It was also completely

inappropriate as we are total strangers. In my experience, this type of invitation would be a setup for a sexual encounter and assault. It was definitely NOT received as perhaps you might have intended and was very disturbing.

My concern is that there are other male survivors you have met in your years of work that have experienced and interpreted your words and actions in similar ways and were left feeling like I did but were intimidated to mention it because of your highly recognized role among our healing movement. Your actions and words now force me to put you on notice that, especially at "survivor." gatherings, you cannot assume that your own sense of love and sharing love is comfortable and freeing for survivors like me - IT IS NOT!

Finally, I believe you're smart enough to fully understand what I detailed above, that you will take to heart my attempt to correct your approach in addressing sexual assault survivors, male or female, from here forward. You need to consider how a sexual assault survivor receives, interprets, and feels about YOUR discussion or expressions of "love." I guarantee it is far from what you intend."

Hank Estrada

Despite not hearing from the Male Survivor Executive Director regarding this confrontation letter, I did received the following response from Samuel:

"Dear Hank,

First of all, I am so sorry, out of my heart, I am so sorry. Please forgive me. Please do not put me on notice, and I WILL LEARN from this and NEVER ever do it again. I HEAR your feelings...I will not do this ever again and THANK YOU for letting me know. We all need to learn...I NEED to learn, I am sorry , and I will look into this and change; putting me on notice feels uncomfortable. I have learned from my mistake from you BEING OPEN! Thank you for being OPEN; I will learn from this.

I NEVER EVER MEANT IN THE WAY YOU FELT UNCOMFORTABLE WITH. I just mean LOVE and have been that way forever...I am so sorry; I hear your feelings, and they are true for you. I completely acknowledge them and understand where you are coming from. I do, and never ever do it again in the survivor world. Please forgive me, and I will learn from this and really acknowledge your feelings... I never ever meant any harm."

It's important to note that I also shared this experience with several other survivor professionals at the conference, and they, too, did not seem interested or concerned and simply chose to change the subject. How sad and discouraging this was, knowing that no one I told at this international conference against abuse and victimization seemed to care or even know what to do about confronting and stopping inappropriate behavior by one attendee upon another. Their inaction clearly defeats their life's mission and work to end sexual abuse and victimization. If we can't confront these types of inappropriate and abusive behaviors among our colleagues, then we shouldn't be promoting one's efforts or attempts to end sexual assaults and abuse. We can and must do better.

1in6 Organization's Anti-Demonizing Policy on Sexual Predators

Another nationally known male survivor organization that has propelled itself in the last decade is 1in6.

They, like the Male Survivor organization, have tons of online resource links to help survivors find healing and maintain a highly visible standing among male survivor resource organizations. To my surprise, I received a rejection of UnHoly Communion for inclusion onto their list of recommended books for survivors. The surprise was not that the book was rejected but more so for a reason. According to the email I received from then 1in6, Inc. Executive Director, Steve LePore, UnHoly Communion could not be recommended due to a description of sexual predators as "unforgivable monsters." The following is the actual email I received from Mr. LePore;

"Hank, good morning. Again, I'm sorry for the delay, but as I said in June, there was a long line of books to be reviewed in the queue in front of yours. Additionally, I'm sorry to tell you that the committee is not recommending your book for inclusion in our lending library based in part on their comments below:

The book does not meet our selection criteria because of the way it uses demonizing language to

refer to people who sexually abuse children. While we can understand that he and some others who have been victimized, given where they are in their healing process, may continue to view all who sexually abuse children and have not yet confessed and sought treatment as "absolutely unforgivable monsters," we cannot recommend to others a book that strongly promotes that view.

I wish I had better news for you.

Sincerely,

Steve LePore, Executive Director

1in6, Inc.

I wonder if this censorship of using negative descriptions, i.e., unforgivable monsters, in reference to perpetrators is enforced at every 1in6 support gathering? Survivors should be aware of this 1in6 rule that disregards an otherwise understandable reaction in a survivor expressing negative labels upon those who have assaulted us. I am concerned for an uninformed survivor, seeks support from the 1in6 organization who would gather up the courage to express a similar label about his own perpetrator, only to be reprimanded and silenced. How re-traumatizing it would be for this survivor to be told that the term they use to refer to their perpetrator is inappropriate and not permitted.

In my opinion, this 1in6 organizations book selection criteria banning "demonizing language" that refers to sexual predators may unintentionally give the impression that 1in6 favors equal concern, empathy and respect for perpetrators as for their victims.

Lastly, it would be wise to investigate, research, and seek out however many personal recommendations you can find on every local, national and international survivor organization you might call upon for support and services. These have been my experiences, and I felt it important to raise the awareness that some survivor support resources, individuals, and organizations may not be appropriate to healing.

Chapter 22

Advice for Parents

With regards to parents and how they can help prevent sexual abuse, they must listen to their children and communicate through honest discussions. Look for signs of unusual behavior, such as a new fear of people or places that were not previously feared. Parents should be aware of changes in school performance, attendance, study, and eating habits. In general, any sudden, suspicious changes or mood swings—including depression, violence, and aggression—or the need to avoid social gatherings may signal that something serious has happened.

Parents must continually provide an atmosphere of trust and openness. They should strive to demonstrate a willingness to discuss any subject that their child initiates, no matter how uncomfortable it might be. Even just expressing their discomfort or lack of knowledge with certain topics, such as intimacy or sex, are huge steps towards the healthy development of a child's confidence. Children should also be made to feel free to talk with their parents without fear of judgment, reprimand, or ridicule.

Parents should also educate their children about their right to say "no" to an adult if they are made to feel afraid or uncomfortable by a particular individual. Children need to be taught to recognize appropriate and inappropriate touching or expressions of affection, regardless of who it is. Many of these awareness programs now exist in our communities and can be found through local mental health agencies and hotlines.

On the community level, parents should inform themselves on issues of child abuse prevention. They can request that the subject be discussed at local community gatherings, parent and teacher school meetings, and especially through educational church programs. Parents can write or phone local government representatives on the need for more public funding to establish child abuse prevention programs and victim-assisted services for both adults and children.

Parents should be mindful of the consequences when choosing appropriate measures to discipline children. If there is any doubt in a parent's mind about the appropriateness of a particular disciplinary practice they use, they should check with professional counselors. What was once considered acceptable disciplinary practices in the "old days" might be grounds for child abuse prosecution today.

Lastly, speaking of the "old days," there's no doubt that women are also guilty of being sexual abuse perpetrators and being a nun or member of the clergy does not exclude them from committing the same-sex crimes against children. The old way of thinking is that sexual predators were exclusively men; but clearly, there are no longer any gender exclusions as we learn of more and more horrific stories about female predators. However, here again, we are faced with a long-held prejudice: when women are involved with boys, the boys are not perceived as being victims of abuse. When the offender is a person in the religious life and is also a woman, it's impossible to tell that she is an abuser because it's unthinkable and unbelievable magnitude.

Although we have not heard as much media coverage about the the reality of female perpetrators of abuse, I am personally aware of a number of men who had been sexually molested as boys by women, including mothers, teachers, nuns, and neighbors. By now, we have become painfully aware of the fact that no profession, no matter how sacred they may appear, are immune from the problem of sexual predators are acting out their sexual interests and desires. Sexual molestation of children is criminal, immoral, and evil, regardless of who the perpetrator is.

Advice for Non-Survivors

I have met many "non-survivors," those who did not experience child sexual abuse growing up, and they ask how they should respond to survivors. For many people, especially non-survivors, the subject of child sexual abuse causes a high level of discomfort. As survivors, we are very much aware of this; we know these feelings are unavoidable. But those who are not "survivors" should be conscious of the element of privilege a survivor gives to them in choosing to reveal their intimate story.

The non-survivor is being given the status of trust that is not granted to just anyone. The listener should be aware of this. It's best for the listener not to give advice or opinions nor make critical judgments, even though the urge to do so is strong. The exchange tends to be more productive if the non-survivor simply listens and offers reassuring support.

Listeners can also share what they are genuinely feeling in an honest and sincere manner. For example, if at a loss for words, the listener should just say so rather than remain silent. Silence in this situation could be interpreted as rejection. Under no circumstances should the survivor be advised to just "forgive and forget" the abuse. Such well intentioned advice can be emotionally damaging and patronizing. Be aware that most of us cannot "forgive" and it is impossible for us to ever "forget."

Another ill-advised response that often causes further distress for survivors are to be told, "Pray and give it over to God," or "Pray and He will help you." I can't tell you how many nights I'd pray to God, as a boy alone in my bedroom, to save me, only to have the assaults and violence continue. Suggesting that survivors, years later, just need to pray can "re-victimize" them because it implies that God will now answer prayers, or that God would have saved me from being molested if I had called upon Him sooner and prayed harder. These references to prayers and protection simply cannot wipe away the years of unanswered pleas for help during our moments of molestation and abuse.

175

As children, many victims of abuse spent countless hours praying to be "rescued" and were disappointed, myself included. I am not saying that prayer is not a valid tool in recovery; it has helped many. Placing a sectarian value judgment, however, on the shoulders of a victim/survivor is neither realistic, supportive, or a helpful approach.

Survivors & Humor

I believe most survivors have both a serious and humorous side to their personalities. Some of us use the silly and playful approach to distract us from looking directly at something that may be affecting us emotionally. We thrive on the attention we are able to generate when being humorous and seemingly carefree. It seems as though when we experience a positive response from others like laughter, we feel accepted and "normal." When others appear to be enjoying our antics, we feel like we "fit in."

The only concern I have about this is that with this type of distracting behavior, those painful issues in one's personal life may not be getting the attention and resolution necessary for healing. I am suspect of a survivor who constantly has to be telling jokes or performing "tricks" or laughing for no particular reason, especially when it's inappropriate and awkward.

On the other hand, being extremely serious and never smiling or laughing can be equally as uncomfortable as well. As a child, I learned to take everything encountered very seriously and with great distrust. I have often been told by friends and family to "lighten up" or "chill out." due to my easily becoming distressed and overwhelmed. I learned very young that I needed to organize everything around me, including my own behavior, and always to be prepared for the worst. I am definitely a person who sees the glass as half empty rather than half full. I just never knew what I could do to prevent my father from becoming angry and violent. It seemed impossible to prevent his attacks, no matter how much I tried to control my surroundings and behavior.

Because of the constant threat of danger and violence in my life, I was unable to know how to relax or have fun and play, as other neighborhood children seemed to be able to do naturally. Consequently, as an adult, I am sometimes uncomfortable around people I don't know who are having fun, telling jokes, or acting silly.

Gradually, I have been able to overcome some apprehension with patient encouragement and support from people who understand. I'm always faced with the challenge of letting go of my own personal awkwardness around people playing and having fun. I know I have much more work to do personally in my life in order for me to relax, play, and laugh more.

It's a little easier to "let our guard down" and experience something pleasurable or fun when we are able to surround ourselves with supportive and trusted friends. I have learned that, in my own life, I will always have to push me just a bit more than others to overcome the occasional awkwardness of not feeling playful or funny when it might be perfectly appropriate in an enjoyable social situation. It is possible for survivors to experience fun and laughter wherever and whenever we can, but we have to search for learning opportunities that encourage laughter and having fun.

CHAPTER 23

ROOTS OF CELIBACY

What most people fail to realize is that the practice of mandating celibacy for clergy had more to do with protecting the vast wealth and power of the Roman Catholic Church than spirituality. Concern mostly over the loss of church lands to heirs of priests led to the imposition of the celibacy rule. Pope Pelagius made new priests agree that their offspring could not inherit property. History has recorded that throughout the Middle Ages, Catholic clergy were married to wives and fathered children. Long before the Middle Ages, since before Biblical times, multiple female partners for males, including clergy, had been the norm. For a time in the church's early history, it was acceptable for a Catholic priest to have multiple wives and even mistresses.

The celibacy issue had nothing to do with morality but was ultimately about protecting church money and church property. Making marriage unacceptable for a priest and celibacy, a rule was a slow and purposeful process. In 1022 Pope Benedict VIII banned marriages and mistresses for priests, and in 1139 Pope Innocent II voided all marriages of priests, and all new priests had to divorce their wives.

Middle Age gnostic influences taught that the body was dirty and unspiritual and that to be more spiritual, you had to avoid natural sexuality. The church managed to incorporate this in pious defense of celibacy for its entire clergy from then on.

In the first century, Peter the first Pope and the apostles that Jesus chose were, for the most part, married men. In a passage from the New Testament, Matthew 19:12, celibacy sounds optional. Jesus said, "There are some who have given up the possibility of marriage for the sake of the Kingdom of heaven. Let the one who can accept it, accept it."

In the second and third centuries, during the Age of Gnosticism, the idea that light and spirit are good, and darkness and material things are evil, gave rise to the perception that a person cannot be married or sexually active and be perfect. Celibacy then became that which set the priesthood apart from all other men and was, therefore, a priest's chief means of attaining a spiritual life of physical purity and holy perfection.

Over the centuries, through various Pope and religious councils, some interesting decrees were introduced. These sometimes extreme, sometimes disturbing policies reflect the mindset and practices of a religion and church manipulated throughout the centuries by a few corrupt and power-hungry men.

What follows below are just a few of their contributions to the The Catholic religion, briefly listed according to year: Fourth century—The Council of Elvira, Spain, decree #43: A priest who sleeps with his wife the night before Mass will lose his job.

325 — The Council of Nicea: After ordination, a priest could not marry.

352—The Council of Laodicea: Women are not to be ordained. This suggests that before this time, there was the ordination of women.

385—Pope Siricius left his wife in order to become pope and decreed that priests may no longer sleep with their wives.

401—St. Augustine wrote, "Nothing is so powerful in drawing the spirit of a man downwards as the caresses of a woman."

580 — Pope Pelagius II: His policy was not to bother married priests as long as they did not hand over church property to their wives or children.

590 to 604—Pope Gregory "the Great" said that all sexual desire is sinful in itself.

836 — St. Ulrich, a holy bishop, argued from scripture and common sense that the only way to purify the church from the worst excesses of celibacy was to permit priests to marry. Council of Aix-la-Chapelle openly admitted that abortions and infanticide took place in convents and monasteries to cover up activities of uncelibate clerics.

1045—Pope Boniface IX dispensed himself from celibacy and resigned in order to marry.

1074—Pope Gregory VII said anyone to be ordained must first pledge celibacy: "Priest [must] first escape from the clutches of their wives."

1095—Pope Urban II had priests' wives sold into slavery; children were abandoned.

Fourteenth-century—Bishop Pelagio complains that women are still ordained and hearing confessions.

Fifteenth-century—50 percent of priests are married and accepted by the people.

1545 to 1563—Council of Trent states that celibacy and virginity are superior to marriage.

1517—Martin Luther

Seventeenth-century—Inquisition, Galileo, Newton

1776—American Declaration of Independence

1789—French Revolution

1804—Napoleon

1882— Darwin

1847—Marx, Communist Manifesto

1858— Freud

1869—First Vatican Council; infallibility of pope declared.

1930—Pope Pius XI: Sex can be good and holy.

1962—Pope John XXIII: Vatican Council II; marriage is equal to virginity.

1966—Pope Paul VI: Celibacy dispensations.

1978—Pope John Paul II: Puts a freeze on dispensations.

1983—New Canon Law

1980 — Married Anglican/Episcopal pastors are ordained as Catholic priests in the U.S.; also in Canada and England in 1994.

2007 — Pope Benedict XVI: "Politicians supporting abortion rights issues will be excommunicated from the church," "Gay

clergy will not be tolerated in the priesthood," and "Catholicism is the only true way to salvation." Popes who were married:

St. Peter, Apostle

St. Felix III 483–492 (2 children)

St. Hormidas 514–523 (1 son)

St. Silverus (Antonia) 536–537

Hadrian II 867–872 (1 daughter)

Clement IV 1265–1268 (2 daughters)

Felix V 1439–1449 (1 son)

CHAPTER 24

CONFERENCE OF CATHOLIC BISHOPS

The National Review Board for the Protection of Children and Young People established by the USCCB (United States Conference of Catholic Bishops) produced "A Report on the Crisis in the Catholic Church in the United States" for public release. The following statistics were identified among their findings:

US clerics accused of abuse from 1950–2002: 4,392

About 4 percent of the 109,694 clergies serving during those 52 years.

Individuals making accusations: 10,667

Victims: 5.8 percent under age 7; 16 percentages 8–10; 50.9

percent ages 11–14; 27.3 percentages 15–17

Victims' gender: 81 percent male, 19 percent female

Duration of abuse: 38.4 percent of victims said all incidents occurred within one year; 21.8 percent said one to two years; 28 percent two to four years; 11.8 percent longer.

Victims per priest: 55.7 percent with one victim; 26.9 percent with two or three; 13.9 percent with four to nine; 3.5 percent with ten or more.

Abuse locations: 40.9 percent at priest's residence; 16.3 percent in church; 42.8 percent elsewhere.

It must be noted that 30 percent of all accusations referenced in the USCCB reports were not investigated and were deemed unsubstantiated or because the accused priest had died. Unfortunately, however,these initial numbers are likely to be the only official accounting ever offered to the public by the Roman Catholic Church. Most of the figures listed above are widely suspected to be grossly underestimated, and as soon as the report was published, the USCCB acted swiftly to cut the National Review Board's legitimacy and importance. Initially, this preliminary report was to be followed with the inclusion of audits and a larger, more detailed report issued. The time and urgency for this final report to be presented has long passed and will probably never again be attempted.

Settlements & Costs

In recent years, the Catholic Church hierarchy has had the unavoidable task of facing victims/survivors, families, and parishioners with monumental acts of contrition and financial compensation. By now, most people who followed the news remember that in July 2007, the largest total payout ever by a Roman Catholic archdiocese was awarded to more than 500 plaintiffs in California. At that time, the Archdiocese of Los Angeles agreed to pay between $600 and $660 million in clergy abuse settlements.

In 2004 the Diocese of Orange, California, settled 90 claims for $100 million. The Catholic Diocese of Portland, Oregon, settled its clergy abuse claims for approximately $129 million, and in the Archdiocese of Boston, where the clergy sex abuse crisis originally surfaced, paid settlements to victim/survivor plaintiffs totaling $157 million. In the United States alone, the combined settlement payments to clergy abuse, survivors had totaled over $2 billion, and numerous more follow to this day.

Reports indicate that of the 195 Catholic dioceses in the United States, almost all have faced more than a few clergy sexual abuse claims. Several dioceses, among them Tucson, AZ, and Davenport, IA decided to seek bankruptcy protection. In addition to these enormous case settlements by various archdioceses throughout the U.S., several prominent Catholic religious orders, i.e., the Carmelites, the

Franciscans, and the Jesuits, have each reached a multi-million dollar settlements with plaintiffs who were sexually assaulted by members of the order.

There have been well over 100,000 cases of sexual abuse by clergy in the United States alone, and we can only imagine what horrors exist in religious communities and parishes outside the U.S. What untold evil practices by unsupervised clergy in socially and economically desperate countries we yet to uncover? How many more unseen victims of clergy sexual abuse are right now being threatened, assaulted, or worse, permanently silenced?

The ultimate "slap in the face" by the Catholic Church today, has been the fact that some parishes are actively soliciting donations from congregation members to help pay for settlements to victims by their own clergy. Local parish communities have sought and filed for bankruptcy, claim to have sold off church-owned real estate, and even shut down parishes in shameless attempts to feign financial hardships forced upon the church by survivors, thereby deliberately contributing to a new, unspoken prejudice and contempt for outspoken survivors of clergy abuse. This tactic, like that of protecting pedophiles and sexual predator clergy will ultimately come back to haunt them.

I have chosen to expose Father John Raab, CMF, the Claretian Missionary Order, and the Catholic Church as I experienced them, and I believe that there are many more religious organizations, communities, and churches throughout the world that have unknown numbers of pedophiles, sexual predators, and victims living among them.

I want readers to understand the real probability that pedophiles and sexual predators know how to blend in with any group, organization, or community. And when someone's behavior seems suspect with regards to inappropriate and unwanted touching, "red flags" should immediately be raised that may signal real sexual predator threats and danger. Pedophiles and sexual predators live everywhere within many societies, religious organizations, and neighborhood communities.

Their unknown identities among us remain a serious threat, not only to innocent, trusting children but also to millions of vulnerable adult survivors now. The disturbing reality is that pedophile and sexual predator mindsets will never disappear from our societies or stop being threats. Now more than ever, we need to be vigilant and proactive in the fight to stop sexual predators and their assaults in whatever legal way each one of us can.

Although my experience clearly addresses the crisis within the Catholic Church, there remain other religious denominations that have also had to confront their own sexual predator realities.

Consider a few of the following:

The Center for Domestic Violence once reported that 12.6 percent of clergy said they had sex with church members. And 47 percent of clergywomen had been harassed by clergy colleagues.

The Presbyterian Church stated that 10 to 23 percent of clergy have "inappropriate sexual behavior or contact" with other clergy and employees.

The United Methodist research (1990) showed 38.6 percent of ministers had sexual contact with church members and that 77 percent of church workers experienced some type of sexual harassment.

The United Church of Christ found that 48 percent of women in the workplace have been sexually harassed by male clergy.

The Southern Baptists claim 14.1 percent of their clergy have sexually assaulted members.

Because of the Catholic clergy sex abuse crisis, we all have to realize that it's up to each one of us to demand accountability from those who portray themselves as religious, moral authorities but fail to prevent sexual assaults by known predator clergy. A zero-tolerance for all sexual predators (clergy and non-clergy) is necessary to ensure and maintain the safety and well-being of current, as well as future, generations.

185

CHAPTER 25

GOOD CLERGY DISCLAIMER

I want to say here that as in every social class, community, and organized religion, there are good and not-so-good members. Within the Catholic Church, there are truly honest, loving, and morally sound clergy members living and working among unknown sexual predators who have managed to remain hidden. We shouldn't disregard the sincere life vocations of good priests and another clergy because of those sexual predators who are still protected by a corrupt church its spiritual leaders.

Believe it or not, some of us have been able to hold onto positive, fond memories of other priests and religious clergy who have inspired us in sincere, loving, and nurturing ways. I believe there are priests and religious who have and will remain positive spiritual leaders for the faithful followers who choose to stay. I am also pleading with these good clergy members to publicly join survivors, their families, and parishioners whenever possible to challenge known church officials who have lied and failed to protect children from sexual predator clergy. Simply put, to remain silent and passive is to condone the crimes your sexual perpetrator brothers continue committing. Live the life that Christ himself preached: protect children, for God's sake! I would also like to add for the record that I myself have been inspired by a few genuinely trustworthy, faithfully committed, morally sound clergy in my own lifetime. These honest, celibate men and women of faith are spiritual role models despite current overwhelming suspicions by the general public and inspired me to always find hope even in the darkest moments of despair.

I have very fond memories of social gatherings, formal and informal, where various members of the clergy lovingly consoled individuals in times of grief and pain. I have also been present when a a particular member of the clergy captivated an entire room of people with stories, humor, and hearty laughter. For me, these priests are true examples of Jesus Christ's presence in the world today. I found myself wanting to follow their example of Christ's love and compassion because I believed they held a confident sense of spirituality and faith and seemed to have a sincere connection to a God of hope, compassion, and love.

I have stayed in contact with several priest friends and, ironically, now find myself offering them my support and consolation amidst the seemingly unending sexual predator priest crisis. They tell me they have noticed subtle distrust, suspicion, and even disgust by members of their own congregations and parish communities. They are feeling unfairly judged simply because they are Catholic priests or members of the clergy. I have heard, and continue to hear, about ever-increasing sense of disappointment and despair due to known sexual predator clergy continuing to be defended, even protected, by various official religious representatives, including Pope Benedict XVI himself.

Church Future

My response to my clergy friends is that they are experiencing what most family members of sexual perpetrators experience guilt by association, suspicion, avoidance, and isolation. When all is said and done, as long as survivors of clergy sexual abuse are further silenced and punished by large institutions like the Catholic Church and leaders like Pope Benedict XVI, I believe suspicions are valid when claims of absolute moral authority are proclaimed as justification for immoral behavior.

In my opinion, this sexual predator clergy crisis will continue because the Catholic Church is ignoring its own secret history of dysfunctional sexual practices, and making impossible attempts to "police" its own known and yet unknown pedophile clergy members.

I continue to be amazed at the absolute blind trust that both Christian and Catholic parishioners continue to place upon their clergy, despite warnings by those of us who have experienced life-changing sexual assaults by similarly prayerful, dynamic, authoritative, and influential priests.

I recently recall watching a local Catholic TV program and hearing the host priest excitedly express to the attending audience that "we lovingly embrace everything our beloved Pope Benedict says and asks us to do." "No questions asked" was the implication and the entire audience stood up and applauded in agreement. I was left to ask, "How can this undeserved trust still thrive?" I find this unbelievable, especially in light of what we now know regarding the Vatican's policy of protecting pedophile priests, the vicious legal tactics implemented against victimized parishioners and their families who came forward seeking compassion and justice, as well as the arrogant cover-ups by trusted church leaders.

If we continue to place our trust in spiritual leaders blindly, no matter how high their position, and do not question their spiritually inspired doctrines that result in absurd, un-Christian treatment of fellow human beings, then we are sure to experience an even larger, equally devastating crisis.

The Catholic Church's deliberate concealment of clergy sexual predators and the serious threat they pose on others was morally wrong from the get-go and most educated, free-thinking, spiritually grounded citizens agree. However, predator clergy are counting on those spiritually faithful, blind, emotionally detached followers who, despite overwhelming physical evidence, I do not want to believe that this hellish evil still may exist among some of their current priests and parish communities.

Similarly, nor would these followers ever think of disobeying or disagreeing with a member of the clergy, even if that clergy member's behavior or words seem inappropriate It's such followers that allow predator clergy to continue preying on innocent victims while hiding behind personal denial, naiveté, and most dangerous of all, apathy. Some church members will stand by Holy Mother Church, no matter what scandal or crisis may arise. Some, like myself, will forever distance ourselves from "organized" religions like the Catholic Church, because of its centuries of deliberate concealments of sexual abuse crimes and heartless disregard for human life.

Unfortunately, my hopeful opinion of the Catholic Church's ability to "do the right thing" changed when I learned of the sinister and brazen attempts by church officials to silence victims and their families from seeking help. For this, I am deeply ashamed and resentful of anyone who knew about and protected pedophiles or sexual predator priests. There is no amount of settlement money or public apologies from the Catholic Church that will ever make up for decades of clergy sex assault crimes and organized cover-ups.

In my opinion, there remains an unmitigated atmosphere of secrecy, superiority, and arrogance among members of large organized religious organizations, including the Catholic Church, and I do not realistically expect to see this change unless people of faith start to consistently demand accountability and change.

In 2020, a new Associated Press (AP) investigation found that almost 1,700 Catholic priests and staff accused of child abuse live freely in the US, with no oversight from law enforcement or church supervision. The AP found that since they were accused, 65 have been charged with a variety of crimes, 76 have licenses to work in schools or medical establishments, and only 85 charged with sex crimes are registered sex offenders. More than 130 dioceses in the US have publicly named priests, deacons, monks, and worshippers accused of historic child abuse since August 2018. The discovery was part of a broader investigation into the whereabouts of 5,100 priests, deacons, monks, and laypeople in Roman Catholic Churches in the US "credibly" accused of child sexual abuse dating back decades.

CONCLUSION

This overwhelming crisis is everywhere and worldwide, but a the solution has begun right here and right now, each time a survivor courageously speaks out. I recognize that as someone who had no intention of ever telling my humiliating secrets, and so publicly on an international level, I've managed to impart hope, courage, and change for other survivors in ways I may never completely know. I will always carry childhood, and now clergy, sexual assault histories with me but by breaking my silence, I heal just a little bit more and help others feel less helpless and alone.

With each passing day, I have learned to accept the pain and sorrow I experienced as a sexual assault survivor, as being in its rightful place, IN THE PAST. I know I can slay my emotional and psychological dragons when they resurface and realize that I'm forever in the process of burying the negative remains.

I'll continue to speak publicly against the brutal realities of sexual assault upon children and vulnerable adult survivors. I have made it my life's focus and work to help other survivors, particularly men, find courage and hope beyond their own sexual assault traumas. I'll continue to support and encourage survivors on their journey towards healing, and at every opportunity, acknowledge those survivors who do not become offenders in their adult lives but instead become protectors and defenders of the innocent. I have no unrealistic expectations about seeing an end to child and clergy sexual abuse in my lifetime. Sexual predators of all types will continue to abuse as long as they believe their secrets are safe with victims and people chose to defend and protect them.

Sharing my personal experiences here with you in this book remains for me yet another means of healing and moving forward.

Hopefully, you too will discover something similar that will provide you with knowledge, insight, hope, and courage for your own life's journey towards inner peace and healing.

I am fortunate enough to have the unconditional love of a wonderful life partner who came from a loving, supportive non-abusive family and could see past my personal misery and pain. Since September 11, 1983, Antonio and I have joyfully celebrated our years together, and I can honestly say that I know the healing power of unconditional love. I am loved not simply in words alone but in our entire relationship and life experiences. I live every day feeling immeasurable love, respect, understanding through my partner's patience, support, and wonderful sense of humor. I am genuinely able to embrace each of them. It is from this love that I find my courage, confidence, and inner strength to speak out against all sexual predators and those unforgivable church leaders and their consciously blind followers who still protect them. I welcome your support and invite you to stand with me now.

Antonio and me.

192

REFERENCE RESOURCES

History sources:

J. N. D. Kelly and Michael Walsh, Oxford Dictionary of Popes, 2006.

Henry C. Lea, History of Sacerdotal Celibacy in the Christian Church, 1957.

Edward Schillebeeckx, The Church with a Human Face, 1985.

Links:

www.bishop-accountability.org

www.snapnetwork.org

www.hankestrada.com

ABOUT THE AUTHOR

Hank Estrada is an internationally recognized spokesman, author, activist, and pioneer advocate for non-offending adult male survivors of child sexual abuse. A graduate of Loyola Marymount University in Los Angeles, CA. In 1986, he founded P.L.E.A. (Prevention, Leadership, Education, and Assistance), the first national non-profit organization to assist non-offending adult male survivors and those who care about them. Hank continues to inspire healing from his home in Central New Mexico by exchanging his expertise, support, and compassion with anyone seeking to heal from sexual molestation and abuse trauma.

At home in New Mexico

www.ingramcontent.com/pod-product-compliance
Lightning Source LLC
Chambersburg PA
CBHW061305110426
42742CB00012BA/2065